# FAMOUS
# AMERICAN
# TRADEMARKS

## Arnold B. Barach

PUBLIC AFFAIRS PRESS, WASHINGTON, D. C.

Published by Public Affairs Press
419 New Jersey Avenue, S.E., Washington, D. C. 20003
Copyright, 1971, by The Kiplinger Washington Editors, Inc.
Printed in the United States of America
Library of Congress Catalog Card No. 72-177402

# INTRODUCTION

Look at any successful business catering to the American public. Ask what are the ingredients of its success and you will usually find they include a good product, competitive prices, capacity to meet a broad-based public need, production and managerial know-how—*and* a trademark that rings an instant bell of recognition in the potential customer's mind. You see the words Pepsi-Cola or Coca-Cola and you think soft drink. Arrow or Hathaway means a man's shirt. Campbell is practically a synonym for soup, while Del Monte conjures up a picture of canned fruits and vegetables. The Travelers Insurance Company's umbrella, Sinclair Oil Company's dinosaur, Chevrolet's parallelogram, American Telephone and Telegraph's bell, and dozens and dozens of others have truly become part of the American vernacular and one responds to them as old and comfortable friends, and that is the way their owners like it.

I remember a trip I took some years back to the desert area that lies beyond the Atlas Mountains in Algeria. We had stopped at a small Arab village which looked as if time had never caught up with it—one suspected it had not changed in 2,000 years. An enterprising camel driver persuaded us to try a ride on his docile animal. No sooner had we mounted the beast when a young urchin darted out from nowhere, pointed his box camera at us and (uttering the only English words he knew) shouted "Kodak, Mister?" What better evidence could one ask than that Kodak had truly become an international word meaning "to photograph," "to take a picture"?

In that same village we were invited into one of the mud-encrusted huts, there to view an interior absolutely primitive in its furnishings and facilities—except for two testimonials to modern living: a rusted and bent Singer Sewing Machine Company sign that hung askew in a corner; and a nonticking alarm clock with the words "Big Ben" still visible on its

iii

face. In that remote spot, both trademarks produced a sudden nostalgia for home.

The use of symbols or words to identify products has its roots very early in the industrial revolution in England during the 18th and 19th centuries. The "hall mark" impressed by goldsmiths and silversmiths of that period on their bowls, pots and other pieces to identify the maker was in a way the grandparent of all "trademarks." Of the actual names and symbols still in use, the oldest is generally acknowledged to be Crosse & Blackwell, a food-packaging firm whose brand name was initially used in England in 1706 and imported to the United States 120 years later. Its continued use to this day provides a sort of immortality to founders Edmond Crosse and Thomas Blackwell, who professionally were chefs to the English nobility.

Other trademarks and brand names of equally impressive lineage can be seen in the stores and trade marts of the world: Josiah *Wedgwood* and Joshua *Spode* china, originated in 1759 and 1770 respectively; the *Encyclopaedia Britannica* (1768); *Gordon's* gin (1769); *Mallory* hats (1817); International Silver's *"Rogers Brothers"* brand (1847). As the years progressed, the list became more and more crowded, and by 1881 it was obvious to U.S. lawmakers that chaos and bitter court fights would rage if steps were not taken to protect the owners of trademarks against copycats and imitators. That year the U. S. Patent Office registered its first trademarks; since then it has listed over 900,000 different ones in the books. The registration is good for 20 years and is renewable at the option of the owner at 20-year intervals for as long as he sees fit to use it.

For years it was practically axiomatic that a product's success could be measured by the degree of public recognition of its trademark. The respected and instantly recognized name or symbol was as likely to produce buyer acceptance as anything else the marker emphasized—price, quality, design or whatever. People regarded the familiar brand as a dependable brand, and most still do. Usually, and only for the most persuasive reasons, such as economy, do they turn to the unknown or little-known. No matter what the product—cars,

TV sets, or neckties—everything else being equal, the "name" brand with its familiar symbol or label is the one likely to get the business.

So it is little wonder that businessmen guard their trademarks with jealous proprietary possessiveness. And well they must, for otherwise the trademark's exclusiveness can slip away and the name may take its place as just another word in the language. The records are replete with examples of the penalty of carelessness. Sidney A. Diamond, a respected legal authority on such matters, lists aspirin, cellophane, celluloid, escalator, kerosene, lanolin, linoleum, milk of magnesia, shredded wheat, and thermos as examples of trademarks that have entered the public domain because the rules of ownership were ignored.

These rules are well-tested and explicit. A trademark must identify a brand of a product, but it cannot be a substitute for the name of the product. Therefore, it is not a noun but a proper adjective (always used with a capital letter). A company does not identify a Whiz-Bang washing machine as just a Whiz-Bang. If it does that often or recklessly, the trademark will lose its legal standing. There are exceptions, of course. You may see a car advertised as a Pontiac (not a Pontiac car) or a cigarette brand as Salems (not Salem cigarettes), but that's because the makers are satisfied that their dominance of the market with these trade names is so complete as to be unchallengeable even by someone who would dare to try to duplicate or imitate the trademark.

Other rules have to do with display of the trademark, an indication (usually with a small R in a circle) that it is registered, and thorough indoctrination of employees, admen and others involved in its use that it is a trade name, that it describes the company or product that owns it, and that absolutely never can it be used to refer to someone else's widget, gadget or anything else.

How is a trademark—word or symbol—created? That is one of the fascinations of the business. The answer is there is no standard pattern. Whim, public competition, scientific survey, childhood memory, sudden inspiration, middle-of-the-night revelation, contrived nomenclature, a man's or woman's name or face—all have been the route to trademarks whose value is immeasurable. Hotpoint, Gerber, Band-Aid, Coca-Cola, O.N.T., Sunbeam, Life Saver plus innumerable others came into being almost by accident or by one person's offhand suggestion. Today, their proprietors can only shudder at the mere suggestion that the business might try going it without them.

This book brings together the stories of these and dozens of other well-known trademarks and symbols. Most of them are still in use; a few have been changed or replaced. The lore, the history, the legend, and even the human personality in their creation and development are told essentially in the light of information furnished by the owners themselves. There is humor in some of the stories, sober comment in others. But together they represent fascinating chapters about an aspect of American business about which little is generally known.

In addition to the corporate symbols, here and there are the stories of trademark equivalents that have played vital roles in the development of social and governmental institutions— names such as Mr. Zip, Smokey the Bear, the Olympics triad.

All of these stories originally appeared in a continuing feature of *Changing Times*, a magazine published by the Kiplinger Washington Editors, Inc. They have been put together in this volume with the hope that they will be of interest to the public at large.

ARNOLD B. BARACH

*Washington, D.C.*

# CONTENTS

| | | | |
|---|---|---|---|
| A & P | 1 | FORMICA | 65 |
| AMERICAN EXPRESS | 3 | FRUIT OF THE LOOM | 67 |
| AT & T | 5 | GERBER FOODS | 69 |
| ARM & HAMMER | 7 | GILLETTE | 71 |
| ARMCO | 9 | MGM's LION | 73 |
| BABY RUTH | 11 | GOODYEAR | 75 |
| BAKER'S CHOCOLATE | 13 | GREYHOUND | 77 |
| BAND-AID | 15 | HALLMARK | 79 |
| BICYCLE PLAYING CARDS | 17 | JOHN HANCOCK | 81 |
| BIRDS EYE | 19 | HARTFORD'S HERT | 83 |
| BLUE CROSS | 21 | HATHAWAY'S SHIRTS | 85 |
| BON AMI | 23 | HEINZ | 87 |
| BURMA-SHAVE | 25 | HEMINWAY'S KITTEN | 89 |
| BUSTER BROWN | 27 | HERSHEY'S CHOCOLATE | 91 |
| CAMPBELL SOUP | 29 | HOTPOINT | 93 |
| CANADA DRY | 31 | HOWARD JOHNSON'S | 95 |
| CANNON TOWELS | 33 | KELLOGG'S ROOSTER | 97 |
| C&O's CHESSIE | 35 | KILOWATT | 99 |
| CHEVROLET | 37 | KLEENEX | 101 |
| CHIQUITA BANANAS | 39 | KODAK | 103 |
| COATS & CLARK | 41 | LEA & PERRINS | 105 |
| COCA-COLA | 43 | LEVI'S | 107 |
| CO-OP | 45 | LIFE SAVERS | 109 |
| CRACKER JACK | 47 | MAXWELL COFFEE | 111 |
| DINERS CLUB | 49 | METROPOLITAN LIFE | 113 |
| DUTCH BOY | 51 | MOBIL | 115 |
| DUTCH CLEANSER | 53 | MORTON SALT | 117 |
| ELSIE THE COW | 55 | NABISCO | 119 |
| ENCYCLOPEDIA | | OLYMPICS | 121 |
| BRITANNICA | 57 | OSCAR | 123 |
| FISHER BODY | 59 | PALMOLIVE SOAP | 125 |
| FISK TIRES | 61 | PARAMOUNT | 127 |
| FLORISTS TELEGRAPH | 63 | MR. PEANUT | 129 |

| | | | |
|---|---|---|---|
| PHILIP MORRIS | 131 | SQUIBB | 163 |
| PHILLIPS 66 | 133 | SMOKEY THE BEAR | 165 |
| PILLSBURY | 135 | STATE FARM INSURANCE | 167 |
| PROCTER & GAMBLE | 137 | SUNBEAM | 169 |
| PRUDENTIAL INSURANCE | 139 | SUN-MAID | 171 |
| QUAKER OATS | 141 | TOOTSIE ROLL | 173 |
| RALSTON'S PURINA | 143 | TRAVELERS INSURANCE | 175 |
| REVERE | 145 | UPJOHN | 177 |
| SAFEWAY | 147 | WEBSTER COLOPHON | 179 |
| SALADA TEA | 149 | WESTINGHOUSE | 181 |
| SAMSON CORD | 151 | WHITE OWL | 183 |
| SANTA FE | 153 | WHITE ROCK | 185 |
| SCOTCH BRAND | 155 | WHITMAN'S CHOCOLATES | 187 |
| SHERWIN-WILLIAMS | 157 | WOOLMARK | 189 |
| SINCLAIR | 159 | MR. ZIP | 191 |
| SMITH BROTHERS | 161 | | |

George Huntington Hartford was an Augusta, Maine, youth who struck out to make his fortune and wound up in New York City back in 1859. Like every fortune seeker, he had an idea. His was to take advantage of the national craze for tea by buying it by the clipper-shipful and selling it at dockside for one third the going price.

The initial shipload was a roaring success, and with the profits Hartford opened a store on Vesey Street, in downtown Manhattan. It was painted bright red and gold, and its cashier's cage was built in pagoda style. On Saturday nights a brass band played to draw in the trade. But all this was merely box-office trappings to achieve Hartford's true purpose: sale of food at discount prices. Coffee was added to the line, national magazine advertising was launched, and Wells Fargo wagons went up and down the land distributing the company's wares.

In 1869 the first transcontinental rail line was completed at Promontory, Utah. Hartford knew that phenomenal business expansion — including his own —

would follow in the wake of the coast-to-coast rail service. He was shrewd enough to exploit the public fervor over the goings-on at Promontory. What better name for his prospering stores than "The Great Atlantic & Pacific Tea Co."?

Actual establishment of stores on the West Coast came after Hartford's death in 1917. Today the food chain, largest in the world, counts thousands of units in its operations, plus a multitude of satellite businesses such as bakeries, a fishing fleet, canneries, coffee plants and — yes — tea distributors. As far as the public is concerned, only one possession has shrunk: its name. To most people, The Great Atlantic & Pacific Tea Co. is now just plain and simple A & P.

No nobleman of ancient Rome knew what it was to carry a traveler's check on his journeys or a credit card for easy admission to the Baths or the latest spectacular at the Colosseum. Metal coins were his currency, and the reigning Caesar their guarantor.

Today, a symbol of ancient Rome still is inscribed on the currency of travelers and shoppers, only this time it's stamped not on coins but on strictly non-Roman conveniences: traveler's checks and credit cards.

The American Express Company's symbol on its credit cards and "cheques" (American Express favors the English spelling) is a stern-visaged Roman, member of an elite cavalry corps that reached its eminence during the glory of the Republic and, later, the Empire. Eventually, the corps became the training ground for Rome's leading financiers and capitalists who developed the intricate trade patterns of the known world.

The symbol was chosen in 1950, the creation of an artist named A. E. Foringer—famous for a Red Cross World War I poster that produced $150,000,000 in contributions—who used live models for his work. The identity of the individual who posed in the helmet with the horsehair crest is unknown. The artist died

3

shortly after his original painting was completed.

The trademark's principal function is to serve as an anticounterfeiting weapon. During the 1940's, the company suffered severely at the hands of counterfeiters. Now, says the company, the trademark helps make its checks and credit cards practically immune to counterfeiting. Thus, the resolute cavalryman of glorious Rome again serves as protector against those who would trespass on the public's statutes.

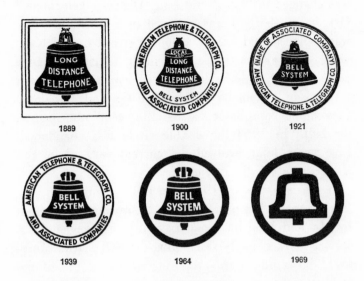

1889    1900    1921

1939    1964    1969

Symbol of a man, a service and the nation's biggest utility—that's the blue bell. The man was Alexander Graham Bell. The service is phone communication. The utility is American Telephone & Telegraph Company.

Angus Hibbard, first general superintendent of AT&T, thought up the blue bell. He tells the story in his autobiography, *Hello—Good-bye*:

"We wanted a sign for Alexander Graham Bell's telephone. With that as the fundamental, I sketched on paper the outline of a bell. To the next question, 'What kind of telephone are we to advertise?' there was but one answer, the long distance telephone. And so I printed within the outline of the bell the words 'Long Distance Telephone.'"

The symbol—called a service mark—was approved January 5, 1889. By 1895, when local equipment was interconnected with long-distance stations, the lettering was changed to "Local and Long Distance Telephone." Originally, the bell was enclosed in a rectangle. This was replaced in 1900 by a double circle, in which the name of the company was printed. Another change came in 1939, with the double circle enclosing the words "American Telephone & Telegraph Co. and Associated Companies," and the legend "Bell System" inscribed on the bell. In 1964 the double circle was abandoned. Five years later evolved the current very plain and modernistic wordless symbol.

A crisis arose in 1953 when the phone company learned that a Washington, D.C., answering service, run by Mr. and Mrs. Raymond L. Smith, had registered a service mark strongly resembling the Bell mark. Moreover, the Smiths were proposing to license use of the mark to other answering services around the country, with the wording "The Bell Answering System" in the double circle. To its horror, AT&T discovered that nobody in the company had ever bothered to register the Bell System mark! Beyond doubt, the Smiths were within their rights.

A deal saved the day. AT&T paid $18,000 to the Smiths. The Smiths thereupon abandoned their mark and AT&T proceeded to institute registration of the Bell System insignia against all future infringement.

Originally, the Arm & Hammer trademark was used to identify the spice and mustard products of a company called Vulcan Spice Mills, which at the time of the Civil War was located on Furman Street in Brooklyn. James A. Church, the young man who owned the mill, chose the symbol because in Roman mythology Vulcan was the god of fire, skilled in fabricating weapons for the gods and heroes. The symbol depicts the brawny arm of Vulcan about to strike an anvil with a hammer.

Young Church was the son of Austin Church, who owned Church & Company, a baking soda manufacturer. In 1867, James joined his father, taking along his Arm & Hammer trademark. Church at that time sold baking soda under various names. In a few years, it was found that people selected the Arm & Hammer package and, in due time, most of the other labels were dropped.

A competing brand was sold under the "Cow label," adopted in 1876 by John Dwight, a relative of the Churches. They competed in cousinly fashion until 1896, when the two companies were merged, becoming the present Church & Dwight Company.

Cow Brand Baking Soda is still favored by people in Connecticut, metropolitan New York and in a few communities along the Missouri River. Elsewhere people buy the Arm & Hammer brand. But while the labels are different, the bicarbonate of soda inside is exactly the same.

Sometimes original trademarks become victims of growth and expansion, and remedial action must be taken. That was the dilemma with Armco Steel Corporation, which early in its history adopted a triangle as its trademark, symbolizing employes, management and customers — "a triangle of effort welded firmly together in the spirit of quality and service." The triangle was originally a double-dotted line, with the words "American Ingot Iron" along each side. Then it was changed to a solid line, with "Armco" across the face. This version became familiar to readers of the *Saturday Evening Post* and other popular magazines in the 20's as the company pioneered steel ads in the consumer press.

Confusion came as the company grew. It organized or absorbed such subsidiaries as Armco International Corporation, Sheffield Steel Corporation, Armco Drainage & Metal Products, Incorporated, National Supply Company and Union Wire Rope Corporation. Its business volume topped the billion-dollar-a-year mark. It employed over 40,000 people in steel plants, mines, quarries, sales offices, warehouses, manufacturing plants. By 1959 the corporation had 102 letterheads in

9

use, each one different and—together with a multitude of different packages, plant signs, business forms, etc.—representing a hodge-podge of corporate identification.

So in 1961 the old inverted triangle was redone in a modern concept. The name Armco (for the company's original name: American Rolling Mill Company) breaks the triangle in half and is sharp and clear, a switch from the previous curved and hard-to-read version.

Baseball fans notwithstanding, any rumor that the Baby Ruth candy bar was named for the home run king has no basis in fact. The name honors a White House baby, the eldest daughter of President and Mrs. Grover Cleveland, born between his first and second terms and endearingly referred to as "Baby Ruth."

Curtiss Candy Company selected the name for its nut roll candy bar after it was suggested by an employee in a naming contest. The nut roll had been called Kandy Kake when introduced by Curtiss several years after the company was organized. It was in the early 1920's that founder Otto Schnering figured that Baby Ruth on the label could enable him to outdistance his competitors. (He was right. Standard Brands, which now owns the company, says Baby Ruth has long been the top-selling nut roll bar.)

The trademark was patterned exactly after the engraved lettering of the name used on a medallion struck at the time of the Chicago World's Columbian Exposition in 1893. The medallion pictured the President, his wife and daughter Baby Ruth.

To get the candy bar known, the company gave away hundreds of thousands of samples in Kankakee, Illinois, South Bend, Chicago and other midwestern cities. It hired airplanes to drop bars suspended by tiny parachutes over Pittsburgh (creating a 1924-style traffic jam). It organized a 26-plane aerial circus, a Scottish Kiltie Band, hockey and bowling teams and a six-pony team that toured the country boosting the candy. In the depths of the depression a penny version of the Baby Ruth bar was introduced, but that bargain is no more.

## BAKER'S CHOCOLATE GIRL

La Belle Chocolatière was an Austrian maiden
(Anna Baltauf) who married an Austrian prince in
1745. For a wedding gift, the prince presented her
with a pastel portrait of herself by Jean-Etienne Liotard,
a well-known Swiss artist. Because Anna had been a
waitress in a little Viennese chocolate shop when the
prince met her, he had her pose in her waitress's uni-
form.

The portrait acquired a fame of sorts, ultimately
finding its way into the Dresden Art Gallery. Meanwhile, in 1764, a man named Walter Baker had established a small chocolate mill on the Neponset River
in Dorchester, Massachusetts, just outside Boston. Looking about for a suitable trademark for chocolate and
cocoa, Baker adopted La Belle Chocolatière as practically made-to-order for the job.

The Viennese chocolate girl has adorned every package of Walter Baker's Breakfast Cocoa and other

products for two centuries. The corporation, a part of the General Foods Corporation since 1927, is proud that as early as 1777 its cocoa was sold with a money-back guarantee, and that it was the only packaged and nationally-advertised food product sold in Abe Lincoln's general store in New Salem.

The cocoa and other chocolate products are still milled on the banks of the Neponset. As for La Belle Chocolatière, her portrait was returned to the Dresden Collection after being hidden during World War II. The East German communist government used the occasion to turn out a postage stamp depicting "Das Schokoladen-mädchen," proving that the Reds can make political capital out of a 200-year-old romantic tale of a prince and a maid.

Like most new brides, Mrs. Earle Dickson, of New Brunswick, New Jersey, soon learned that hot pots and pans produced nasty burns on delicate hands. Sharp knives and other utensils inflicted painful nicks and cuts in spite of all precautions. Her husband gave her more than sympathy—he devised a quick way to provide relief from cuts and burns. In the process, he assured himself of business success.

What Earle Dickson did was take a strip of surgical tape manufactured by his employer, Johnson & Johnson, and lay it sticky-side up on a table. Then he rolled a pad of gauze bandage, stuck it on the middle of the tape and covered tape and gauze with crinoline. Now, his bride's problems were over. If she ever cut or burned herself, she simply cut off a slice of the bandage, whisked off the crinoline and applied the patch.

Upon hearing of this ingenuity, Dickson's co-workers steered him to the front office. Johnson & Johnson executives were quick to see the possibilities. They began to make the new product, but they had no name for it until W. Johnson Kenyon, superintendent of the mill, came up with Band-Aid.

Band-Aid adhesive bandages found a place in the nation's medicine chests, hospitals and first-aid kits.

15

Since its beginning in 1920, the trademark has embraced a constantly expanding array of first-aid and surgical products, including sheer and plastic strips, spots and patches, nonstick bandages, surgical closures, plastic tapes, spray-on antiseptics, etc. The products sold under the Band-Aid trademark today account for a good share of the 1.5 billion adhesive bandages sold annually.

Earle Dickson benefited well from his ingenuity. When he retired in 1957 he was a Johnson & Johnson vice-president—propelled up the executive ladder by his wife's complaints.

Everybody knows a playing card is not a bicycle, and yet 40,000,000 bridge addicts plus uncounted millions of card players more often than not use Bicycles. It is easily the nation's best-selling brand of playing cards.

Bicycle Playing Cards were christened by a printer named August M. Berens, who was just trying to help out the boss. Berens worked for Russell Morgan and Company, a Cincinnati printing firm. In 1884, 14 years after its founding, the company went into the playing card line. In 1885 it came out with a new pack but lacked a brand name. Gus Berens said why not name them after the current technological marvel, the bicycle. So Bicycle the brand became. (In the company and in the trade the brand is called just plain "Bikes.")

The word itself was almost as new as the cards it described. It didn't exist until 1869, when English inventor J. I. Stassen coined it to provide a one-word description for his two-wheeled vehicle. Never did he imagine that his bicycle would label one of the indispensable ingredients of bridge parties and poker games.

Bicycles (now made by Russell Morgan's direct

descendant, United States Playing Card Company) are produced in two types: poker or standard deck and bridge deck (a quarter-inch narrower). Both are available with "jumbo-indexes" for the bifocal set. They are sold with either red or blue backs and are distinguished by their Victorian design—curlicued backs featuring six winged cupids, two of them engaged in the improbable pursuit of riding a bicycle.

Clarence Birdseye, his wife and infant child were living in subzero Labrador in the winter of 1916 and apparently enjoying it except for one small lack: they yearned for a regular diet of fresh vegetables and other fresh foods. When the supply ship brought in fresh items on its infrequent visits, Birdseye—who was there on a fish and wildlife survey for the U. S. government —tried preserving them by dropping them in barrels of freezing water. On being thawed out, the vegetables tasted almost as good as the originals. So did fish and caribou meat.

Birdseye, inventor and entrepreneur as well as adventurer and explorer, saw real commercial potential in the idea. He would go back to New York, perfect a quick-freezing process, and get rich. His first venture, Birdseye Seafoods, began operations six years later in New York and lasted a few months. His next venture, located on the Fort Wharf in Gloucester, Massachusetts, where the fishing boats came in, was more laboratory than factory. But when Mrs. Marjorie Merriweather Post, then head of the Postum Company (predecessor of General Foods), happened by on her schooner, the *Hussar*, and tasted Birdseye's frozen products, the inventor had a supporter. General Foods bought Birdseye's patents and trademarks in 1929 for $22,000,000, of which Birdseye got about $1,000,000. His brokers shared the remaining $21,000,000.

What happened to Clarence Birdseye? He died in 1951 with a succession of other inventions to his credit, including a marker harpoon for whales that is still used. He never minded that chopping of his name in half to make a trademark. In fact, he used to say that was the way it was spelled originally, in honor of an ancestor whose well-aimed arrow pierced the eye of a hawk that threatened an English queen. The queen thereupon dubbed him Bird's Eye.

## THE BLUE CROSS SEAL

If you're one of the millions of people who belong to Blue Cross, check your membership card and you'll find this trademark, squeezed down to about two-thirds the size of a dime.

The design is an adaptation of the Geneva or Greek Cross, internationally recognized as meaning help for the sick and wounded.

It dates back to 1934, five years after a trailblazing hospital insurance plan was organized for Dallas schoolteachers by Justin Ford Kimball, himself an educator. Another educator, E. A. van Steenwyck, created the original Blue Cross trademark to publicize the Hospital Service Association of St. Paul, of which he was the director. The association was modeled after the Dallas plan.

In a very few years volunteer prepayment hospital insurance plans all over the country had adopted the Blue Cross, and by 1939 it was official. That year the American Hospital Association became the trademark's official custodian, zealously controlling its use. On the Blue Cross was superimposed the AHA seal.

As for the seal, if you could actually make it out, you could see that it includes just about every emblem known to the medical profession plus a number of other things:

The Caduceus has for centuries symbolized the healing arts.

The Cross of Lorraine has meant relief to the unfortunate since the Middle Ages.

The Urn Lamp, symbolic of knowledge, is the official emblem of the Florence Nightingale nurses.

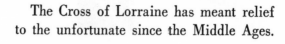

The Maltese Cross has been used for centuries by the Saint John Ambulance Service, named for the Knights of Saint John of Jerusalem.

Maple Leaf,
for Canada

American Eagle,
for U.S.A.

Geneva
Cross

Finally, the Latin motto *Nisi Dominus Frustra,* "Without God we can do nothing."

## BON AMI CHICKS

Inventors are rarely good advertising men, and the inventor of Bon Ami was no exception. He was an ingenious Connecticut farmer named John T. Robertson, who discovered that feldspar added to a cake of soap made a fine abrasive that would clean without scratching. He dubbed his product Robertson's Mineral Soap and took to his buggy to sell his product door-to-door.

The year was 1884. In seven years, business was thriving, and Robertson had acquired a factory and seven stockholders. That's when Robertson's promotional approach came under criticism. The product's name, said the stockholders, was all wrong. It required too much space in small ads. Besides, it didn't go well with the company's expansion plans. Since the main customers at the time were French-Canadian housewives, the soap should be given a name meaningful to them. Thus was born Bon Ami—or Good Friend.

The "Hasn't Scratched Yet" line came a couple of years later when the company's first paid advertising-promotion man, Louis H. Soule, looked for a slogan with real punch to get across the soap's scratchless quality. What better way to dramatize the slogan than a picture of a newborn chick just out of the shell?

Name, slogan and chick have over the years appeared on the company's cake soap and powdered cleanser. In addition, Bon Ami has been used on other products such as Jet-Spray and Dust-N-Wax.

*The draftee tried a tube and purred,*
*Well, whaddya know, I've been deferred.*
*Burma-Shave.*

Every motorist has seen Burma-Shave doggerel along
the highways: six signs in a row, 100 feet apart, usually
in a rented field, the "verses" varying from the punny
(above) to the ridiculous (below):

*Men with whiskers 'neath their noses,*
*Oughta have to kiss like Eskimoses.*
*Burma-Shave.*

The 18-inch by 40-inch signs, bolted securely to
protect them from souvenir hunters, represent what is
one of the most original advertising ideas of all time.
They date back to September 1926, when the first set
("Cheer up, face—the war is over! Burma-Shave")
appeared on U. S. Highway 65, near Lakeville, Minnesota. Today thousands of verses dot the landscape,
many of them contributions of individuals who compete every two years for prizes ranging from $2 to $100.
The jingles are changed annually.

Burma-Shave is the product of a Minneapolis manu-facturer who started business with a liniment dubbed Burma-Vita (meaning life, or vigor, from Burma) be-cause three of the essential oils—camphor, cassia and cajuput—come from Burma. The word Burma was retained when the company marketed a shaving cream.

As for those verses, they make friends because they entertain. And friends, hopefully, become customers. Some jingles preach safety:

*Passing cars when you can't see*
*May get you a glimpse of eternity.*
*Burma-Shave.*

And some are accepted but later censored in the interest of good taste. Example:

*My man won't shave, sez Hazel-Huz,*
*But I should worry—Dora's does.*
*Burma-Shave.*

## BUSTER BROWN

Buster Brown and Tige received top billing in the comic strips years before they were purchased as a trademark by the Brown Shoe Company, makers of Buster Brown shoes. The rambunctious Buster and his pup were as famous as Li'l Abner in their funny paper heyday around the turn of the century.

One of the regular readers of the strip was a young man who worked for Brown Shoe, John A. Bush. In 1904 Bush dreamed up the idea of converting Buster Brown and Tige to a trademark—probably the first such tie-up in the history of advertising. He sold the idea to his company, then persuaded R. F. Outcault, creator of the comic strip, to go along. Bush, who subsequently became chairman of the board, saw over $30,000,000 spent on promotion of Buster and the dog.

From the initial exhibit in 1904 at the St. Louis Exposition, the trademark has been represented by real-life midgets and dogs in shoe stores and local theaters, advertised in magazines and newspapers and over network radio and TV, to say nothing of posters and cutouts used in thousands of stores around the country. Contemporary small fry have been exposed to Buster via the "Captain Kangaroo" show.

Not an eyelash of boy or pup has been altered over the years. Bug-eyed Tige still smiles canine fashion and wears the enigmatic number 5 on his collar, while pie-hatted Buster with his page-boy haircut still winks.

A Philadelphia lady named Grace Gebbie Drayton created the Campbell Kids. Only she didn't call them that. She was just having a lot of fun (and making a little pin money) by drawing "mischievous, roly-poly, fun-loving" twins as party favors for friends and others. Completely unexpected fame came when some people from the Campbell Soup Company saw the drawings and made a deal with Mrs. Drayton to adapt them for car-card advertising.

That was in 1904. A year later, in September 1905, the Kids showed up in a Campbell ad in the *Ladies' Home Journal,* and from that day to this they have been used in every type of advertising and promotion imaginable, have been collected in scrapbooks by three generations of children, and have done more to sell Campbell's soups, tomato juice, pork & beans, beans & franks, and chile con carne than almost any other advertising gimmick ever dreamed up by the company.

In the early part of the century people saw the twins as drivers and pilots of primitive cars and planes. In World War I they were Liberty Bond salesmen. In World War II they were air-raid wardens. In the 20's they danced the Charleston and in the 50's they lived in frozen igloos (that's when Campbell frozen soups appeared). They have also been used to convey messages about good manners, nutrition, and good home-making.

From time to time, the appearance of the twins has changed to keep in tune with current styles. And their fame isn't just limited to the U. S. They are known everywhere from Haiti to Hong Kong, in over 100 markets where Campbell soups are sold. Favorites vary from country to country. In Latin America, the leader is cream of asparagus. In Scandinavia, it's mushroom. In the Far East, chicken noodle takes the prize. And in Britain, the twins do best in selling ox-tail.

The geographic outline of our neighbor to the north may well be more familiar than that of any nation in the world save our own, thanks to the trademark of Canada Dry. Look closely at it and you will see Hudson Bay, Baffin Bay, the southern tip of Greenland, and some of the Queen Elizabeth Islands reaching toward the Arctic. If this conveys refreshing coolness, that's exactly what the trademark's designer, J. J. McLaughlin, intended.

McLaughlin was a Toronto pharmacist and "mixer of mineral waters." In 1906 he concocted a carbonated beverage, which he named "Canada Dry Pale Ginger Ale." Besides seeking a reputation of refreshment for his beverage, he wanted to suggest superiority over its competitors. So he added a crown to the trademark to symbolize "kinglike quality."

In the early days the shield contained emblems of the Canadian provinces, plus a crouching beaver (which, along with the maple leaf, is Canada's national emblem). These touches were dropped as the company grew. Ultimately, shield, map and crown constituted a trademark that is recognized from supermarket to swanky bar.

31

McLaughlin prospered, partly because of the almost immediate popularity of his beverages in the U. S. By 1923 his heirs were ready to sell out. The company was bought for $1,000,000 by P. D. Saylor and J. M. Mathes, who founded the present Canada Dry Corporation.

With the sale went the trademark, which today identifies more than 100 different flavors plus a growing line of alcoholic beverages.

TRADE MARK
MADE IN U.S.A.

CANNON

Sell towels with an artillery piece as the trademark? Few modern advertising experts would consider the idea as worthy of second thought. Yet a North Carolina textile weaver decided it made good sense and created a prospering towel, sheet, blanket, bedspread and stocking business as testimony to his judgment.

The man's name was Cannon—James William Cannon. He was the founder of Cannon Mills, which he established in the Reconstruction days in Concord, North Carolina. It was Cannon's idea that there was money to be made in the manufacture of yarn closer to the cotton fields than was then the practice. A little later, he foresaw greater rewards in the weaving of cotton cloth. To this he gave the name "Cannon cloth." From cloth to towels was but a short step, and the sale of towels soon eclipsed the sale of Cannon cloth.

Cannon realized that his towels needed a label that could neither be washed off nor pulled off. Trouble was, no machine existed that could sew a label on the company's products. So the idea was put on the shelf.

To Cannon's son Charles—who took over the presidency of the company after his father's death—goes credit for developing the sew-on label. He located the needed machine in the early 20's and promptly adopted his father's idea of using the cannon trademark. Simultaneously, he launched the first consumer advertising campaign in the textile industry.

The trademark's cannon was a famous field piece in its day. It's a howitzer, appropriately called the "Napoleon howitzer" because the Corsican adopted it for his Russian campaign. Later on it became a mainstay of Civil War artillery regiments who never imagined that one day the cannon would symbolize a business that was to emerge successfully from the shambles of the Reconstruction.

## CHESAPEAKE'S CHESSIE

A cat may look at a king. It may also practically re-
name a railroad, which is why the Chesapeake and
Ohio is sometimes called "Chessie's Railroad" and its
thousands of miles of track, "The Chessie Route."
Chessie is one member of the feline family whose nine
lives are practically immortal because she became a
corporate symbol.

Chessie's original name was "The Sleepy Cat." It
was under that heading that an etching appeared in the
Sunday magazine section of a New York newspaper in
1933. Animal-admirer L. C. Probert, vice-president
of the C&O, saw the picture, clipped it, and suggested
that it be included in an ad announcing the company's
new air-conditioned sleepers. "Sleep Like a Kitten in
Air Conditioned Comfort" was the slogan. Initial publi-
cation was in the September 1933 *Fortune.*

People wrote in to say how much they liked the ad,
and the company moved fast to get exclusive commercial
rights on the sketch from its creator, Viennese artist
G. Gruenewald. In 1934, the sleeping cat was christened
Chessie, simultaneously with her appearance on the

C&O's now famous Chessie calendars. "America's Sleepheart"—as Chessie was also called—subsequently acquired two sleepy kittens and (naturally) Chessie's Old Man, named Peake, as proud and smug a tom as ever lived.

The family is among C&O's most treasured assets. The railroad boasts that passengers and shippers have been prone to go C&O just because of affection for Chessie and her brood. As a matter of fact, some people liked her so much they sent gifts ranging from catnip to cantaloupes. But the sad truth is, Chessie and her relatives are not and never have been real—they are solely the product of an artist's whimsy.

A Chevrolet and a Ford have this much in common: They are both named for people. In Chevy's case, the name was that of a Swiss-French auto racer, Louis Chevrolet, who had a yen to make automobiles. But, unlike Ford, the man had little to do with the success of the product that bears his name. Louis Chevrolet's cars were big, expensive and built like European racing models, and they didn't sell well.

His backer, a promotion genius named William C. Durant, recognized what the problem was and promptly abandoned Chevrolet's design for something simpler and cheaper. But he retained the name (he liked its musical sound), and he merged the company with another of his enterprises, Little Motor Company. (Durant, incidentally, founded General Motors in 1908, lost control in 1910, regained it in 1916 with the help of du Pont money and finally was forced out for good in 1920).

Durant's first low-priced models came out in 1912. In 1913 came the economy roadster, the Royal Mail, priced at $750, and a touring car, the Baby Grand, listed at $875. Sales soared to over 13,000 in 1914. In 1916 came the "490," touted as a car to be sold for $490, but it never was. Rising costs shoved the price past the $700 mark.

Durant literally swiped the inspiration for the square and parallelogram trademark emblem from the wallpaper in a Paris hotel room. He tore off a sample, brought it back to the States and had his advertising staff go to work on it. It has been a unique feature of the automobile's nameplate ever since.

Probably the smartest marketing idea ever developed to sell bananas was a lighthearted calypso tune titled "Chiquita (little one) Banana." Two songsmiths, Len MacKenzie and Garth Montgomery, wrote the jingle one afternoon in 1944 for the nation's banana king, United Fruit Company. Remember the words?

*I'm Chiquita Banana and I've come to say*
*Bananas have to ripen in a certain way . . .*
*Bananas like the climate of the very, very*
    *tropical equator*
*So you should never put bananas in the*
    *refrigerator. . . .*

From the song came the trademark. And from the trademark came fantastic promotional success—so impressive that United Fruit in 1970 changed the name of its marketing subsidiary to Chiquita Brands, Inc., and is packaging lettuce, celery and other products with a variation of the blue Chiquita seal.

Songstress Patti Clayton was the original Chiquita Banana girl (accompanied by six señores on maracas, jawbone, tom-tom, guitar and bass fiddle). Then came a 24-year-old ex-steno, Elsa Miranda, born in Puerto Rico. Her throaty Latin rendition was equally good in calypso, bolero, rumba, tango, samba and jive.

"Chiquita" starred with the Boston Symphony and on the radio with Bert Lahr, Charlie McCarthy, the King Sisters, Alec Templeton and Ellery Queen. Three times in a row Chiquita bananas were peddled on (Fred) "Allen's Alley." Later came movie commercials and, still later, television.

You don't hear the Chiquita song any more. But if it's ever revived, there will be one change: the line about "never put bananas in the refrigerator" will have to go. United Fruit now says it's okay to refrigerate if you want to stop the ripening process, but, as any housewife knows, you can expect the skins to turn brown.

The sewing machine Elias Howe patented in 1846 had a number of practical drawbacks—not the least of which was that no existing thread could be used with it. Twenty years later, George Clark, a thread manufacturer in Newark, New Jersey, did invent a six-cord thread with the strength and size suitable for sewing machines. He called it "Our New Thread." The thread made the sewing machine a success, and the sewing machine created a market for the thread. Clark shortened the name of his product to "O.N.T." As a trademark it has found a permanent home in the nation's sewing baskets.

George Clark and his brother, William, were grandsons of one of the founders of a Paisley, Scotland, company that had originally supplied loom "heddles" (silk loops to hold the warp in place) to shawl weavers on Paisley's Cotton Street. When Napoleon cut off Britain's supply of silk, the company diversified by developing a twisted cotton thread that was strong enough to replace the silk.

Meanwhile, another Scottish company, J. & P. Coats, also branched out into the thread business. Five years after the Clarks started their Newark mill, the Coats company had a mill in Pawtucket, Rhode Island. It had adopted the circled chain in Scotland as its trademark.

In 1952 the companies merged to become Coats & Clark, Incorporated. In its 11 mills Coats & Clark makes crochet cotton, wool knitting yarns, embroidery floss, zippers and, of course, millions of miles of sewing thread. And on the spool there appears the Clarks' O.N.T. enclosed by Coat's linked chain—though well over a hundred years old, it is still "Our New Thread."

The tale of how a Confederate veteran and struggling pharmacist, John S. Pemberton, concocted the first batch of Coca-Cola syrup in a three-legged iron pot in his back yard is fairly familiar. Not so well known is the story about how the mixture was named. Credit goes to Pemberton's friend and bookkeeper, F. M. Robinson, who saw the appeal of an alliterative compounding of names of two of the mixture's ingredients: coca, the dried leaves of a South American shrub, and cola, an extract of the kola nut.

Robinson inscribed the hyphenated designation in flowing script, and, 85 years later, the name Coca-Cola identifies a product consumed by more people than any other trademarked item.

Coca-Cola's nickname, Coke, was the creation of the beverage's customers, who insisted on it despite early company ads urging: "Ask for Coca-Cola by its full name; nicknames encourage substitution." By the time the company realized the value of the abbreviation, plagiarists had appeared and it took a Supreme Court decision in 1920 to rule that Coke meant "a single thing coming from a single source. . ." The nickname is now a registered trademark, too, and guarded as zealously as the original.

Even so, Coca-Cola and Coke are today the world's most imitated trademarks. Coca-Cola is also the most litigated trademark in the U. S. Competitors galore— only a few of them successful—have attempted to cut into the company's fantastically profitable business.

The curved and fluted bottle, originated over 50 years ago, is almost as famous as the trademarks; in fact, the company regards it as a third trademark. Several years ago Raymond Loewy lauded it as "the most perfectly designed package in use today."

Coca-Cola is now seen around the world, and undoubtedly comes close to Old Glory itself in symbolizing the U.S.A. to millions of people in every corner of the globe.

## CO-OP SYMBOL

The Co-op movement blends high idealism with hard-headed business sense. To its members it represents a way of accommodating the practices of free enterprise to a philosophy that says the owners and patrons of a business can be one and the same.

From its sputtering beginnings in this country in 1798 (by the Shakers), its disciples have seen its fortunes rise and fall and rise again until today U. S. Co-ops count well over 15,000,000 families in their ranks, sharing in a total business volume of billions of dollars annually. They run stores, insurance associations, telephone companies, electric utilities, medical associations, farm supply co-ops; they own such diverse enterprises as a hot water heater factory, oil refineries, seed mills, a serum laboratory and a grease factory.

True to its idealistic concept, the Co-op trademark is saturated with meaningful symbolism. To the ancients, the pine tree stood for endurance, immortality and fertility, and it appears frequently in the myths of the Egyptians, Persians and Indians. It was from them that the Co-ops appropriated it.

Why two pine trees in the Co-op version? Because

it takes two or more of anything to cooperate. The trunks of the pine trees are rooted to the circle—another symbol of eternal life.

Even the colors of the original pine tree symbol had meaning. The trees and circle were in dark green (or chlorophyl green) to indicate life. The background color was golden yellow, the color of the sun—giver of light and life.

With or without color, the symbol is now found wherever there is a Co-op. Its use is jealously guarded. The words "co-op" or "cooperative" cannot be used in a business name unless the organization employing them conforms strictly to Co-op principles. Any nonobserver of this rule quickly finds himself in court.

## CRACKER JACK

You've heard of tea tasters, wine tasters and cheese tasters, but did you ever hear of a popcorn taster? They were around once. Back in the 1890's, F. W. Rueckheim employed them in his popcorn company in Chicago.

One day he made up a popcorn-and-peanuts concoction that he dipped in molasses syrup and formed into semi-sticky clusters for chewing by the handful. He called his tasters for a reaction.

The concoction was an immediate hit. One taster liked it so much he exclaimed: "That's a crackerjack!"

Rueckheim not only respected his taster's good judgment, he also liked his choice of words. Thus the name "Cracker Jack" for the company's new product.

The sailor-boy symbol came along a few years later in a burst of national pride. As the company explains it, "Prior to the first World War, Americans proudly displayed their patriotism and Cracker Jack was no exception." With occasional modernizing to keep him up-to-date, the sailor boy and his dog, Bingo, have been the symbol for the box of candied popcorn and peanuts ever since.

Cracker Jack has two other distinctions: the first wax-sealed, moistureproof package, introduced in 1904 and marking the advent of waxed paper; and the introduction of toy surprises as a sales promotion gimmick.

The company became a subsidiary of the Borden Company in 1965, and Cracker Jack's sales curve has continued its upward hike. Maybe that's because today's kids—like their grandfathers before them—just can't resist the lure of finding something waiting for them at the bottom of the box.

## DINERS CLUB

The Diners Club "split circle" trademark symbolizes (1) the globe, (2) the letters D and C, (3) international traffic signs used in European and other foreign countries, and (4) the carefree life.

The original Diners Club symbol was a classic globe, but this was soon deemed too stodgy and too conventional for an enterprise in tune with modern life and living. So the artist assigned to redesign it produced what the company terms a "strong and individualistic" trademark.

The letters D and C are reversed to enclose the global circle. The stark black design is intended to provide instant recognition wherever it is posted: restaurants, hotels, shops, airlines, on credit cards, in ads, on stationery, etc.—the same kind of instant recognition provided by European traffic signs. In the full-color version, the official "Diners Club blue" is intended to blend global travel and good living by symbolizing access to sea and sky.

The split circle is displayed in about 350,000 "member establishments" scattered, the company says, in 143 countries—everywhere from "Anaheim to Zambia, from Philadelphia to Paraguay." Over 2,000,000 people carry the Diners Club card.

The card claims to be the ancestor of all those of its type. A man named Frank MacNamara had the inspiration for the service one day in 1950 when he forgot his wallet and had trouble paying a restaurant check. From restaurants, use of the card spread to stores, travel agencies, hotels and dozens of other places where the card replaces cash. And used it is, as any card holder can testify when the monthly bill arrives.

## DUTCH BOY

Michael Brady a Dutch lad? That he is, begorra, and he's been one for more than 60 years. Hidden beneath that Dutch haircut of his is a soul as Irish as a leprechaun's—camoflaged by an artist's brush in the interest of selling paint.

A Dutch artist named Yook made the preliminary sketch of the portrait. Another artist named Lawrence Carmichael Earle executed the picture. Young Mike Brady was hired to sit as a model for Earle's portrait.

The portrait solved a troublesome marketing problem for the National Lead Company, which had been created in 1891 out of a merger of 25 makers of white lead scattered from Boston to St. Louis. It had become apparent that national advertising of the new combine's product would be impossible as long as the 25 individual units continued to use their own brand names. Ad manager O. C. Harn thought up the idea of a Dutch boy painter (everybody knew that Hollanders kept

51

things whitewashed, spic and span) as an advertising symbol for all 25 companies.

One of the trademark's claims to fame is its versatility. It is one of the few that can be altered to suit the mood or theme of an ad. The Dutch Boy, for example, has been depicted as an athlete and, in one ad, stood on his head.

National Lead describes the Dutch Boy as "gay, pleasing, loveable, warm, honest," and says this Irish Dutchman (or Dutch Irishman) is "a great little salesman." His haircut is certainly in the contemporary mode.

The year was 1906, and the American housewife's growing concern with cleanliness was opening up new vistas for soap manufacturers. One of the products to appear on the scene was a cleansing powder, somewhat abrasive in content and intended to remove stubborn spots and stains from utensils without excessive use of elbow grease. Its producers called it "Old Dutch" Cleanser to relate the efficiency of the powder to the legendary reputation of spotless Dutch households.

A nameless artist first visualized the trademark of a housewife chasing dirt in her vigil against soiled surroundings. Naturally, he drew her as a Dutch lady, with flowing blue skirts and a heavy hood. In her hand went a trusty stick, a sign of her determination to keep things clean.

The trademark was a familiar sight in the nation's kitchens and cleaning closets for half a century. The old girl appeared on World War I bond posters, her belligerent stance ready-made for the assignment. Before that, in 1912, she had been a tool of satire when "Puck" used her likeness to poke fun at Teddy Roosevelt's trust-busting campaign. Her symbol as a dirt chaser has been used on labels printed in French, Spanish, Portuguese, Chinese and Japanese—but never in Dutch.

Some years back, Purex Corporation, Ltd., bought "Old Dutch" Cleanser from the Cudahy Packing Company, and later changed the name to just plain "Dutch Cleanser." The formula was improved and the package modernized. The dirt-chasing girl was replaced by a slim modern maid with golden hair, gay and happy, wearing a perky white cap and apron, her dress brightened with white collar and cuffs. Thus, the symbol of housewifely brawn yielded to one of dainty—but nonetheless efficient—femininity.

## ELSIE THE COW

Elsie the cow is a purebred Jersey who made her debut 34 years ago as a cartoon character in medical journal ads designed to sell doctors on the virtues of milk. Her success was assured and within a year she had attained national fame through four-color advertisements everywhere. Her sponsors, the Borden Company, knew a money-making bovine when they saw one, and in 1939 produced Elsie in the flesh at the World's Fair in New York. Elsie drooled at the 11,000,000 people who crowded her boudoir, then moved on to greater fame on stage, screen and TV, accepted keys to more than 170 cities, and even accumulated an imposing list of "honorary" college degrees.

But Elsie's enterprising sponsors knew that ultimately their prize would fade unless something sensational occurred. It did. In 1957 Elsie, with the connivance of a crew of public relations experts, produced twin calves to commemorate Borden's first hundred years. A grandmother from Anaheim, California, named them Latabee and Lobelia and thus pocketed a name-finding fee of $25,000.

All through the years Elsie (incongruously known as the "World's No. 1 Milkman") has been presented as a lady of dignity and good breeding, carefully protected against blatant commercial display.

ENCYCLOPÆDIA
Britannica

The thistle, say the experts of *Encyclopedia Britannica*, is "a spiny-leafed plant with a head of rose, purplish, or yellowish, tubular, five-parted flowers seated on a pitted and hairy receptacle, belonging to the Compositac family. It is considered by some to be a weed; by others, a flower."

How, then, does this prickly weed (or flower) come to be the trademark of one of the most scholarly creations among the literary works of man—the *Britannica* itself?

The thistle is the Scottish national emblem, and since the *Britannica* was originally the product of three Scots, constituting "the Society of Gentlemen," what better way to honor them than by adoption of the thistle as the trademark? The three were Colin Macfarquhar, Andrew Bell and the first editor, 28-year-old William Smellie, described by his peers as "a veteran in wit, genius and bawdry."

(It should be noted that Scotland adopted the thistle as its emblem because of an incident—probably legendary—that occurred in a thirteenth-century battle with the Norwegians. Goes the tale: Hakos's army maneuvered for a surprise attack on Alexander II at Largs. One of Hakos's barefooted Norwegian troops stepped on a thistle and yelped in pain, thus betraying his army's position, and enabling the Scots to deliver a devastating defeat upon the Norsemen.)

It wasn't until the fourteenth edition (1929) that the thistle was adopted by the *Britannica*, and then it was used only as a border for certain pages.

The original thistle was a finely filigreed reproduction, but over the years the design gradually became simplified. Over a decade ago the present trademark appeared.

Body by Fisher

Napoleon left his mark on history. He also left one on over 57,000,000 cars, including the Chandler, the Essex and the Maxwell. That mark is the Body by Fisher emblem, riveted to every General Motors car and, prior to 1926, to a long list of now-defunct makes, from the Churchfield and the Oakland to the LaSalle and the Herreshoff. Napoleon gets part credit for it because the design is a blend of two of his more famous coaches—one used at his coronation, the other at his marriage to Marie Louise, Archduchess of Austria.

Adoption of the emblem was presumably the decision of one of the founding brothers of the Fisher Body Company though there is no documentation of this fact or of who first proposed it as a trademark. Also uncertain is the authorship of the classic line, "Body by Fisher." Indisputable, however, is the fact that the trademark went into use on August 1, 1922, and has been on every Fisher body produced since then.

The Fisher brothers had set up shop in 1908. Before long they had an order for 150 bodies from Cadillac. In a very few years the company became the Fisher

Body Division of General Motors and by 1926 it was producing car bodies exclusively for GM.

In 1930 GM organized the Fisher Body Craftsman's Guild. Its purpose was to encourage fine craftsmanship among teen-age boys, who competed for scholarships and cash awards by constructing miniature models of Napoleonic coaches.

Post-World War II teen-agers had little interest in Napoleonic coaches. So the contest—in which over 6,000,000 boys have participated—was concentrated on design and construction of model cars. But this concession to progress has not affected the trademark. It remains unchanged, an auto maker's testimonial to the traditions of the coach craftsmen of old.

## THE FISK BOY

In spite of occasional assertions by gray-haired elders that they posed for the original sketch, the Fisk boy was no one in particular. Back in 1906 the artist, Burr E. Giffen, was a fledgling working for an ad agency known as Wagner and Field. Giffen got the inspiration for the drawing at 3 a.m. one morning, sat down on his bed and rapidly sketched the little boy with a tire over his right shoulder and a candle held in his left hand. Simultaneously, he coined what has become one of the most widely promoted puns in ad history: "Time to Re-tire."

The sketch was a hit with the Fisk Rubber Company, which a few years earlier had introduced its first pneumatic automobile tire. Its initial appearance in an ad was in the March 7, 1914, issue of the *Saturday Evening Post*. Subsequently the tousle-haired, sleepy boy appeared on Fisk cars and truck tires, in ads, on stationery, booklets, posters, calendars, tire store displays and even on clock faces.

Burr Giffen once said he was not annoyed at people who insisted they posed for the original. He suspected they actually posed for one of the many copies executed by other artists over the years and were confused about their true role. But the original sleepy little fellow was strictly a fictitious creation, dreamed up by wide-awake Burr Giffen at three in the morning.

Florists are one-world-minded. They have been that way since before World War I, when a group of U. S. florists banded together under the flag of the FTD (Florists' Telegraph Delivery), and subsequently allied themselves with the British FTD and with Fleurop, an organization of florists in Europe and parts of Asia and Africa.

This international federation—25,000 members in all—has its headquarters in Detroit under the name of Interflora. It has its own currency (the fleurin), used exclusively to simplify international settlements among florists, and dedicates itself to the telegraph, telephone or mail delivery of flowers to almost 200 noncommunist countries, who place no tariff, quota or foreign exchange barriers in its way.

The Mercury banner is used by members in the United States, Mexico, Canada, Puerto Rico, Japan, Venezuela and Panama. Fleurop and the British FTD use one that is somewhat different in design. The current U. S. version is the sixth so far; the original Mercury looked more like a fleet runner than a soaring messenger bearing blossoms.

"Say It With Flowers" was on the trademark for three years (1936-39), but it was no FTD exclusive. It was born in a Boston bar in 1917 where an adman named Patrick O'Keefe was having a drink with Henry Penn, a past president of the Society of American Florists. The two were poking around for a suitable SAF slogan when Penn remarked: "There is nothing you can't say with flowers—when you send flowers, it says everything."

"That's it," boomed the major. "Let's make the slogan: 'Say It With Flowers.' "

Thus was born one of the remembered merchandising slogans of an era—a slogan that can be used by anyone because neither the major nor Mr. Penn thought to copyright their priceless brain child.

# FORMICA®

Ask any housewife what room this trademark suggests, and she'll probably reply, "The kitchen." But if you ask her what Formica is, and she answers "a laminated plastic," she probably took her degree in something like inorganic chemistry.

The word is a manufactured word, and it means just what it says: "for mica." The material got its name because the laminated plastic was originally produced as a substitute for mica in electrical insulation. The producers were a couple of Cincinnati engineers named Herbert A. Faber and Dan J. O'Connor who set up their partnership in 1913 with $7,500 in borrowed capital. To Faber goes credit for coining the "Formica" brand name.

Self-starters for automobiles used great gobs of Formica electrical insulation in the early days. Then came radio and such giants as Freed-Eiseman, de Forest and Atwater Kent who found the laminated plastic ideal for dial and tuner panels. But the material's big conversion to a combined functional and decorative use didn't come until the mid-20's when the company discovered how to seal photographs of various designs in the transparent plastic. Thus was born Formica as the housewife and builder know it.

The big test was during World War II when the *Queen Mary,* generously decorated with the material, went into troop transport service. The plastic laminate came through in fine shape, hardly showing the rigors of wartime action.

If it was good for troop transports, then why not for kitchens? The question came from builders poised for the postwar boom, and the answer was Formica as now used. So while the trademark literally means a substitute for another material, that meaning has long been subordinated to its present identity.

In 1871 the U. S. Patent Office opened its doors to people who had trademarks to register. Among the first in line was Fruit of the Loom. Only 15 years old, it had already demonstrated it had the makings of one of the most original trademarks ever designed.

An apple farmer's daughter provided the spark from which the trademark was created. She lived near the Hudson River in New York State, and she liked to paint pictures of the fruit from her dad's orchard. Her father also ran the local general store. One day daughter happened to lay her latest rendering of a red apple up against a bolt of muslin.

Came a customer, who said: "Please sell me some of that muslin—the one with the big red apple."

Father saw the merchandising possibilities immediately. He put daughter to work painting one red apple after another, which he pasted on bolts of cloth. The cloth with the red apple label became a specialty of the store.

A friend of the merchant-farmer, Robert Knight, of B.B.&R. Knight, Inc., Pontiac, Rhode Island, was the manufacturer of the muslin. Once he saw what the red apple label could do, he adopted it for his entire line, placing it on the first printed tickets used for textiles.

"Fruit of the Loom" was the descriptive line on the trademark. Over the years two clusters of grapes and leaves were added. By 1921 the present version had evolved and in 1938 B.B.&R. Knight (previously sold by the Knights for $16,569,500) became Fruit of the Loom, Inc.

Over 1,000,000 textile items are sold daily with this appetizing label attached. Included are slacks and shorts, bedspreads and tablecloths, pajamas and socks, belts and notions, girdles and bras and hosiery. In all, over 30 trademark licensees turn out about 350 Fruit of the Loom products, giving a long and unexpected life to this amateur's painting of an apple colored red.

## GERBER FOODS

The chores of motherhood were really tedious back in the 1920's. Conforming to pediatric instruction, millions of mothers were spending hours scraping, cooking, mashing and straining the foods spooned into young infants. It was good for baby—but definitely not good for the patience and disposition of their Moms.

Mrs. Dan Gerber of Fremont, Michigan, was one of these exasperated young matrons, and she was lucky. Her husband was in the canning business with his father, and among other things he puréed tomatoes. Mr. Gerber was also lucky. For when Mrs. Gerber asked one day whether "that machine at the plant that purées tomatoes could purée peas for Sally (their baby)," he was launched on a multimillion-dollar business.

Very quickly Dan and his father, Frank Gerber, had a line of five varieties of strained fruits and vegetables for the baby trade. They decided they needed a trademark to symbolize their thriving new line. Top artists and illustrators were invited to submit paintings of a healthy and happy baby. Among the entries was a small, unfinished charcoal sketch of a baby's head, done by an artist named Dorothy Hope Smith.

Asked Miss Smith: Would the company be kind enough to tell her whether this was about the right age and size baby the company wanted? If so, she would be glad to finish the sketch.

The sketch was never finished. The judges felt it had a freedom of line and freshness that would only be spoiled by additional work. It now appears with the slogan "Babies are our business . . . our only business" on over a billion boxes and jars of Gerber food annually. Thousands of mothers send letters and pictures to the company insisting that the sketch is the spitting image of their own little darlings.

*King C. Gillette*

The signature is King C. (for Camp) Gillette. The face
is that of a youngish man, smooth-chinned but luxuriant-
ly mustachioed. The claim to fame is twofold: first, the
"Father of the Safety Razor," and second, the most reproduced face and signature in human history—over
100 billion times at last count.

Young King was a traveling salesman at 21 and, in
his spare time, a tinkerer and an inventor. Why, asked
his friend William Painter, didn't Gillette invent something money-making—something that could be used a
few times and then thrown away? Painter showed it
could be done when he invented the disposable bottle
cap, thus founding the Crown Cork and Seal Company.

One morning, as Gillette struggled with his straight
razor, the dream was born. "In that moment I saw it
all: the way the blade could be held in a holder; the
idea of sharpening the two opposite edges on the thin
piece of steel; the clamping plates for the blade, with
a handle halfway between the two edges of the blade."

It took six years from dream to fulfillment. Gillette hired a young M.I.T. graduate, William E. Nickerson, and it was Nickerson who perfected the idea of the Gillette razor.

The first year of business (1903), 51 razors and 168 blades were purchased. The next year over 90,000 razors and 123,000 blades were sold. By 1906 the business—whose original financing was $5,000—paid out $130,000 in dividends. Since then, over 50 billion blades and half a billion razors have been sold. The portrait and signature trademark has been used on all blade envelopes almost from the beginning.

In recent years the company has diversified into ball-point pens (Paper Mate), home permanents (Toni), men's toiletries and other products. King Gillette, the man behind it all, died in 1932, but his portrait and signature still appear on packages of Gillette blades, testifying that a man can make his fortune just by thinking hard when he faces himself in the mirror in the morning.

## GOLDWYN'S LION

In 1915 young Howard Dietz was an aspiring adman fresh out of Columbia University when he got this assignment: "Dream up a trademark for Samuel Goldfish's new film company."

The company was Goldwyn Picture Corporation, named for Goldfish and his partners, Archibald and Edgar Selwyn. Goldfish, an enterprising immigrant from Poland who later changed his name to Goldwyn, was already making his mark as a Hollywood genius.

Dietz sweated over the assignment, but no inspiration moved him until he remembered that his college humor magazine, *The Jester*, which he edited, liked to titillate its readers by creating small jokes around the college's ancient insignia, a royal lion. The lion dated from the college's early days when it was called King's College, symbolized by a drawing of the regal animal.

Dietz had his inspiration. The lion would be Goldwyn's trademark. An artist named Morris Rosenbaum was enlisted to draw the first Leo—a fine specimen with flowing mane and king-of-the-jungle pose. But Dietz, an erudite young man, decided a final touch was needed —something that would enhance the cultural aura of the Goldwyn company. In Latin, to accompany Leo's roar, he added the motto: *Ars Gratia Artis* ("Art for art's sake").

The Goldwyn company was soon to be swallowed up in a merger, eventually becoming Metro-Goldwyn-Mayer. Over the years dozens of stars shone brightly in MGM's heaven and then faded away as newcomers appeared.

All, that is, except Leo the Lion. You can see and hear him any night at the movies or on TV, the most durable star of all, roaring for the sake of art.

Inventor, businessman and, unhappily, occupant of a Parisian debtors' prison, Charles Goodyear has achieved immortality through the trademark that hyphenates his name with a winged foot. This enterprising Connecticut inventor in his search for the secret of vulcanizing rubber came upon it quite by accident in 1839 when he spilled a batch of India rubber and sulfur on a hot stove. He quickly applied for patents, did business with the U.S. government, fought a series of infringement suits, and finally failed in an attempt to establish a factory in France. That's when he suffered the humiliation of a prison sentence for inability to meet his bills. He died in New York in 1860.

Frank and Charles Seiberling, brothers from Akron, Ohio, memorialized Goodyear when, in 1898, they organized a company to make bicycle and carriage tires, using Goodyear's process. They called it "The Goodyear Tire & Rubber Company" (although Goodyear's descendants had nothing to do with it). Looking around for a suitable identifying symbol, Frank Seiberling got his inspiration from the winged foot on a statue of Mercury that perched on the newel post of a stairway in his home. Mercury was the god of trade and commerce as well as the fleet herald of good news.

Within 18 years the company was the nation's biggest tire manufacturer and, with factories all over the world, today ranks unchallenged as the world's largest tire and rubber company. Diversification of the company has been rapid—it's now in chemicals, packaging, film, flooring, industrial products, footwear, metal products, foam products, aviation, atomic energy and missiles. But the name they bear pays tribute only to Charles Goodyear's inventive genius, not his business acumen.

## THE GREYHOUND STORY

That sleek, streamlined greyhound may be nudging the age of 60. Or then again it may be ten years younger, depending on which legend you believe.

One yarn goes that the name initially was used by a bus line that ran the bumpy route between Los Angeles and Bakersfield in 1912. Another story, better documented, is that the name was the creation of one Frank Fageol, who started operating an intercity bus line out of Muskegon, Michigan, in 1921 under the banner of the Safety Motor Coach Lines.

Several of Fageol's buses were painted gray and, so the story goes, looked so sleek they were dubbed "The Greyhounds." From that, in 1922, came his slogan "Ride the Greyhounds."

Now turn the calendar back to 1914. That year an unsuccessful Hupmobile salesman, Carl Eric Wickman, converted a "Hupp" to a jitney and inaugurated a two-mile bus line running from Hibbing, Minnesota, to the firehouse in the nearby hamlet of Alice. This event marked the historical beginnings of the Greyhound Corporation, though other men and other bus lines were important to the company's development.

Wickman, through the merger-acquisition-consolidation route, helped to form a coordinated system of transportation, the Motor Transit Company. One of the acquisitions was Fageol's Safety Motor Coach Lines, and with that purchase came the greyhound name. In 1930 Motor Transit became the Greyhound Corporation with the "running dog" symbol. And there it has stayed through all the years of growth and expansion into such diverse enterprises as household moving, money orders, tours, food services and industrial equipment leasing.

Once there was a real dog, "Lady Greyhound," who traveled 25,000 miles a year on the promotional circuit. Charmed mayors often presented her with their "leash to the city." Lady retired a few years back and Greyhound's greyhound returned to its status as an inanimate trademark.

Take a product made by a man named Hall. Decide to give it a symbol of quality, good taste, real class. Look for a word that will do for the product what "sterling" does for silver. The word you choose? "Hallmark," of course.

For Joyce C. Hall, founder in 1910 of Hallmark Cards, Inc., the choice was just right. But not until 15 years after he started the business, when greeting card volume began to build up, did he officially designate his line "Hallmark Cards." And not until another 14 years went by, in 1939, did the company begin to advertise its Hallmark cards. Radio listeners of a quarter century ago may remember Hallmark's first sponsored program: "Tony Wons and His Radio Scrapbook." The company was an early convert to television (1951), creating a program of fine drama called the "Hallmark Hall of Fame," which continues to be one of TV's more distinguished—though infrequent—offerings. Plays by Shakespeare, Shaw, O'Neill, Maxwell Anderson, Elmer Rice and others have been shown to audiences that have exceeded 40,000,000.

"People always reach up, never down, for a social

custom," is one of Joyce Hall's pet maxims, so no surprise that he thought well of the proposal to add a crown to the trademark in the late 1940's. Crown and signature go on every one of the 7,000,000 cards sold daily by the company for the happy, the ill, the convalescent, the miserable, the bereaved, the lovelorn, the celebrant and the recipient of holiday greetings.

What's a hallmark? Fourteenth-century English artisans used to put a mark on their products to indicate excellence. They worked in long rooms called halls—thus the term "hall mark." From this, several hundred years later, came a memorable trademark for a man named Hall.

Mutual Life Insurance Company

This is John Hancock's 110th year, and looking back, the company's employes must be startled to learn how close they came to working for a company named Benjamin Franklin Protective Life Insurance Company.

Originally, that was to be the name of the firm, and it was so stated in the notice of intention to incorporate that went to Massachusetts Governor John A. Andrew in 1861. The petition was submitted by a group of 200 Boston merchants and bankers led by Albert L. Murdock, "a man of versatile activities interested in chemistry, mechanics and statistics."

The governor turned thumbs down on the original petition. He had serious doubts as to the workability of several provisions in the articles of incorporation.

A year later, Murdock was back with a new charter, 110 subscribers, $104,000 and a new name: John Hancock Mutual Life Insurance Co. This time all went well, and the company's first agent (Murdock) sold a policy to the company's first customer (Murdock).

Why the switch from Ben Franklin to John Hancock? No one really seems to know.

A compelling reason for the choice was the built-in recognition value of the John Hancock name and signature. First to sign the Declaration of Independence, Hancock had affixed his name with a bold flourish, a fine example of colonial calligraphy. The name "John Hancock" has come to mean signature, and is one of the names in U. S. history deeply imbedded in the public consciousness.

Also, as a quick look at the Declaration of Independence shows, Hancock's signature makes Ben Franklin's look modest—the last thing in the world that a life insurance company's trademark should be.

## HARTFORD'S HERT

What is it? A reindeer? An antelope? A bull moose? A stag, maybe?

A stag it is (an adult male deer). A stag is also called a hart, a fact that explains its fame as the trademark of the Hartford Insurance Group.

Three hundred years ago, seventeenth-century Englishmen called it a "hert," which they pronounced hart. When the citizens of Hertford designed their official seal, they had some fun: They showed a hert crossing a ford. It was a charade so explicit that even the town fool could tell it meant hert-ford or Hertford.

Some years later, a group of Hertfordites migrated to America, taking their seal with them, and founded a new town on the banks of the Connecticut River. The spelling of its name was soon changed to conform to the pronunciation: Hartford. Hartford was to become the capital of the Nutmeg State and the capital of the nation's insurance industry.

The first insurance company in town was the Hartford Fire Insurance Company, parent of today's Hartford Insurance Group. For its trademark it adopted the seventeenth-century Hertford seal.

English artist Sir Edwin Landseer's "Monarch of the Glen," a majestic portrait of a stag, was the model for the century-old trademark. Painted in 1851, it was to be hung in Westminster Palace, but it never got there because the House of Commons was miffed at not being consulted about the artist's fee. An enterprising Britisher bought it, doing a lucrative trade in reproductions, one of which was used in designing the Hartford trademark. Others found their way to saloons along America's western frontiers. This explains why reproductions of "Monarch of the Glen" are occasionally used as props to lend authenticity to saloon scenes in TV westerns.

## HATHAWAY'S BARON

The man in the Hathaway shirt is the son of a former imperial Russian naval attaché, and is descended from a line of Russian and Italian blue bloods, including Count Stroganoff and Duke Sasso Ruffo. As a Russian émigré in Italy, he worked as a travel and hotel man. Later he was a newspaper correspondent in Paris and the U. S., an adman in New York.

In the late 1940's, Baron George Wrangell became a model ($15 per hour), but resisted clothes modeling until Hathaway made a tempting offer. English-born David Ogilvy, former British diplomat and head of the agency with the Hathaway account, is credited with the inspiration for the 50-cent eye patch over the Baron's right eye. It was supposed to provide "overtones of heroism and mystery."

Overtones or no, it was an instant success, and in eight years Hathaway shirt sales almost quadrupled. The Baron's fortunes multiplied with it, and having wed the heiress to the Four Roses whiskey business, he acquired a Spanish villa with 11 servants, a 14-room

New York apartment, and a contract that provides he must work only four months a year.

About the eye patch: It's usually on the right eye. In one series of ads, the patch covered the left eye. Hardly anyone detected the difference.

That "57 Varieties" symbolized by the Heinz trade-mark was the understatement of the century, and no one knew it better than the company itself. At last count Heinz had at least 1,250 different varieties in its roster, with new ones being added almost every week. So little wonder that when the centenary of the founding rolled around in 1969, the firm decided the time had come to rid itself of the "57 Varieties" fiction. It replaced the honored old trade mark with this:

But the "57 Varieties" line was too well implanted in the public mind to be cast completely into limbo. It continues to appear on selected products.

The famous label was dreamed up by founder Henry Heinz a quarter century or so after he organized the firm with L. C. Noble. The story goes that Henry, by 1896 the manufacturer of well over 57 products, was riding a New York elevated train one day when his eye was drawn to a car card promoting a brand of shoes in "21 styles."

"It set me to thinking," he said later. "'Seven, seven'—there are so many illustrations of the psychological influence of that figure. . . . 58 or 59 varieties did not appeal at all to me—just '57 Varieties.'" That's how the phrase was born. A few years later New York's first electric sign, six stories high and a blazing torch with its 1,200 lights, was a brilliant advertisement for the "57 Varieties." At the top, looking almost as good as if it had just been plucked from the barrel, was a Heinz pickle.

There is a suggestion of its ancestral lineage in the shape of the new trademark. The original was derived from the keystone symbol of the Commonwealth of Pennsylvania, birthplace of the company. The new one has the same basic shape except that it's a somewhat squashed keystone.

## HEMINWAY'S KITTEN

Around the turn of the century an alert manufacturer realized that animal pictures attract the public's eye. So he created a furry, mischievous kitten, added a rolling spool to the design and tacked a string of unravelled thread to the spool. Today, millions of home sewers are familiar with this trademark.

The name of the company that promotes the trademark is Belding Heminway and the story behind it goes back almost 150 years to the days when Samuel Whitmarsh from Northampton, Massachusetts, was producing a New England variety of silk thread. In his enthusiasm for Yankee-bred silkworms, Whitmarsh wrote a book that stimulated speculation in silk, thus contributing to the "mulberry panic of 1839" and causing financial ruin for innumerable mulberry speculators, including himself.

Eventually, Samuel Hill picked up the remnants of Whitmarsh's enterprise and named his new company Nonotuck Silk Company. He labeled his thread Corticelli, for a famous Italian scholar, figuring the name would appeal to women who thought Italian silk thread was the best. It was Hill who dreamed up the playful kitten design as the trademark for his product.

A competing silk manufacturer in Connecticut was Merritt Heminway. He had invented the modern wooden spool in the mid-1800's and was the first manufacturer to sell spooled thread.

Four New England farm boys (David, Hiram, Milo and Alvah Belding) were also doing well as silk dealers in Patterson's Mills, Michigan. Together with Corticelli and Heminway, they formed the Big Three of the silk thread industry. In 1926, Heminway merged with Belding and in 1932 Belding Heminway merged with Corticelli (formerly Nonotuck).

About the kitten: It became such a success that it eventually reached Broadway—on an animated sign. Descendants of Whitmarsh, Heminway and Belding recite the legend of how one night wires of the sign got crossed and instead of kitten chasing spool, spool chased kitten.

Occasionally, a name can rise to the top without the power of advertising to propel it. Such a name is Hershey. For years nary a penny was spent to promote its chocolate in the press or over radio and TV.

Not that the company was against advertising. An official once conceded, "We realize the power of advertising, and we have nothing but the greatest respect for it." It's just that Hershey for a long time was able to get along without ads.

Founder Milton Hershey laid down the no-advertising policy. He depended on a good product, an eye-stopping package, a good display and good value for the customer.

An ex-printer's devil, he had a sharp eye for color and design, and the red and black wrappings and labels on his "sterilized milk chocolate" bars quickly gained public acceptance. Around 1903, Hershey switched to the familiar maroon and silver labels printed on flint-coated stock originally imported from Europe. At one time the trademark included a cherub-like child seated in a replica of a cocoa bean and holding aloft a bar of candy or a cup of hot cocoa. This is still used on the company's letterhead.

Milton Hershey made his first million at 43, quit,

tried traveling, got bored, plunged back into business, and ran his million up to 100 times that much. On the outskirts of a Pennsylvania village called Derry he displayed his strong streak of benevolent paternalism by building a complete community for his employes, including four golf courses, an ice arena, recreational facilities for such sports as baseball and tennis, a zoo, banks, a department store, community waterworks— just about everything. The place was called Hershey.

When Hershey died in 1945, at age 88, he left about 70 percent of his chocolate fortune to his favorite undertaking, a school for orphan boys. Apparently the dividends on the Hershey stock have been more than ample to cover all of the school's expenses.

# Hotpoint

As trademarks go, Hotpoint is a very precise one. Originally, it was the name given to an iron whose major claim to superiority derived from its very hot tip. The iron also happened to be the first successful electric one ever made.

It was the invention of Earl Richardson, an Aurora, Illinois, power company superintendent, but its ultimate design was the brainchild of his wife, Mary. Richardson began to tinker with electric flatirons because he figured the electric power business needed something besides home lighting to consume its kilowatts. Around the turn of the century, he came up with his first model. But housewives didn't like it because they said the center of the iron was too hot.

That's when Mrs. Richardson suggested the heat be concentrated in the point of the iron. It would ease the chore of pressing around button-holes, ruffles and pleats, she said. The new design caught on. In 1905 Hotpoint irons outsold every other brand on the market,

Hotpoint's rise was swift, and ads for the company's products appeared in the old *Life, Collier's,* and the *Saturday Evening Post.* In 1918, an historic industrial consolidation took place. The Hotpoint Electric Heating Company and the Hughes Electric Heating Company (originator of the electric range) merged with the heating-device section of the General Electric Company. The merged company's basic products were Hotpoint appliances.

Growth and expansion followed. The company turned out almost every electric appliance known to housewives. But in 1932 it decided to drop small appliances —and out went the electric flatiron.

Twenty years later Hotpoint, Incorporated, became a separately run division of General Electric, and in 1966 Hotpoint appliances and GE appliances were brought under a single management. The Hotpoint name still goes on 500 different appliances—but not one of them is a flatiron.

Yes, there is a Howard Johnson—Howard Deering Johnson, to be exact—and he is the man who originated, built and promoted the national chain of restaurants and motor inns that bear his name.

Johnson was a showman from the start. With an inspiration worthy of Barnum, he began in 1931 to paint the roofs of his establishments brilliant orange to attract passing motorists. Today orange paint has yielded to just-as-orange porcelain roofing tiles.

Shrewd as it was about roof painting, the company didn't recognize its roofs as a ready-made trademark until very recently. A research firm discovered it was one of the best identification tags ever developed. Out went the 35-year-old orange and blue-green Simple Simon and the Pieman trademark. In came the stylized silhouette of orange rooftop and spire.

The new symbol came at a time when the Johnson firm had emerged as the biggest restaurant chain in the world. Johnson started business in 1925, setting up shop in a patent medicine store in Wollaston, Massachusetts, where he made and sold the ice cream that originally brought him fame. From that venture (financed with a borrowed $500), the company grew to its present size of hundreds of restaurants and motor lodges, some company owned, some run by licensed franchisers. It also includes the luxury Red Coach Grills, a chain of "HOJO Junctions," and a line of packaged and frozen foods.

In Colonial days, New England's wayside inns hung symbols over the front portico ("White Swan," "Red Coach," "Watermill," etc.) to identify their establishments. That's exactly what Howard Johnson hopes its orange rooftop does.

## KELLOGG'S ROOSTER

Popped, puffed and shredded, breakfast cereals
make a colorful competitive display on supermarket
shelves, where they take up more space than any other
item. Cereal packages are practically advertisements
in themselves, employing dramatic art and punch-line
copy to capture the shopper's wandering eye. It can
be said of cereal boxes that what's on the outside may
be just as important as what's inside.

That's why the Kellogg Company did not take lightly
the task of redesigning the package symbol for the
granddaddy of all ready-to-eat cereals, Kellogg's Corn
Flakes. Obviously, the choice would have to be a good
one to win attention from all the other corn, wheat,
rice and oats cereals. The company chose shrewdly.
Its happy rooster became as well known as many trademarks that were around much longer.

Why the rooster? The Kellogg people (and ad
agency Leo Burnett Company) chose it because "the
rooster has been greeting the new day since time im-
memorial" and the corn flakes have been "greeting

people at breakfast since the turn of the century." A little on the corny side, perhaps, but a million times a day the rooster is imprinted on a package of Kellogg's Corn Flakes in the Battle Creek, Michigan, plant.

Kellogg's rooster doesn't just crow for corn flakes. The company decided it needed a line to be used in all its advertising—sort of a common denominator sales pitch. The line, originally tied in with the rooster, was "The best to you each morning!"—chosen because "it was, at once, a greeting, a promise and a claim." It was incorporated into printed advertising and has been set to music for radio and TV in the "Kellogg Good Morning Song."

## KILOWATT

Its nose is a light bulb. Its ears are electric out-lets. It wears rubber gloves and shoes. And its limbs and torso consist of four bolts of lightning. Could there be a better symbol to identify intangible, invisible but indispensable electricity?

Reddy Kilowatt was literally born in a flash of lightning. Ashton B. Collins, an official of the Alabama Power Company, had long thought about the usefulness of a symbol to represent electricity as a powerful, friendly, always-on-call servant. One sweltering afternoon in the late 1920's a thunderstorm broke outside his window, and Collins spotted a split-second display of four simultaneous flashes of lightning joined in a brilliant silhouette of arms and legs against the dark sky.

He quickly sketched the rudiments of the new-born figure. Its family name, he decided, would be Kilo-watt. Its first name became Reddy—ready to serve in a flash.

Collins proceeded to organize his own firm, Reddy

Kilowatt, Inc., which owns the trademark and licenses privately owned power companies to use it as their own local symbol. The firm also counsels clients on advertising and public relations. In 1934 Philadelphia Electric became the first to employ Reddy; since then over 200 domestic and foreign power companies have been licensed.

Reddy's assignments are many and varied, from advocating private power in ads to appearing on bill heads that prod delinquent customers.

Kleenex is one of those trademarks that, if the copyright owner isn't careful, could be snatched up into the American vernacular. Like Coke and UNIVAC and Frigidaire, it has close identity in the public mind with a particular type of commodity—but the public doesn't always remember that it's a particular brand. That's why its proprietor, Kimberly-Clark Corporation, has maintained constant vigil to keep Kleenex from joining that growing tribe of ex-trademarks that are now in the public domain—such as zipper, linoleum, cellophane, aspirin, shredded wheat, kiddicar, escalator and thermos bottle.

Every Kimberly-Clark employee is indoctrinated with the rules that preserve the exclusiveness of all trademarks: Always use it as an adjective, never a noun—say "a package of Kleenex tissues," not "a package of Kleenex." It must always be capitalized and spelled correctly. Where possible, indicate that it is registered. Never even remotely imply that the trademark can be used in a generic sense to mean just anybody's tissues.

The Kleenex trademark's origins are fuzzy, as Kimberly-Clark is quick to concede. The company doesn't know how it was chosen or who invented it.

The original tissue product was used as a filter in gas

masks in World War I. After the war it was promoted as a "sanitary cold cream remover." A survey in Peoria showed that the whole pitch was wrong—Kleenex tissues were really favored as substitutes for handkerchiefs.

The sales theme promptly changed. In 1929 came the Pop-Up box. The next year produced a winning slogan, "Don't put a cold in your pocket." Business took off, and while the rest of the nation floundered in a depression, Kimberly-Clark's sales doubled and redoubled.

The company has had thousands of suggestions for other uses of its tissues. It likes to list some on its Pop-Up box, including such unlikely ideas as "Make beautiful flowers from the tissues." One it has never listed came from a customer "who found the tissues ideally suited for blotting up butter drippings when eating corn on the cob."

"A trademark should be short," said George Eastman. It should be "vigorous." It should be "incapable of being misspelled to an extent that will destroy its identity." And "it must mean nothing."

Having established the specifications for a trademark for the camera he invented, Eastman proceeded to create the word to fit them.

Why Kodak? Because, Eastman explained later, "The letter 'K' had been a favorite with me—it seemed a strong, incisive sort of letter. Therefore, the word I wanted had to start with 'K.' Then it became a question of trying out a great number of combinations of letters that made words starting and ending with 'K.' The work 'Kodak' is the result. . . . It became the distinctive word for our products."

In the 83 years since, Kodak has become a permanent member of advertising's international lingo. No nook of the globe is a stranger to its use.

The so-called "Kodak curl," which appears in the corner of the company's ads, had its origin in the 1920's when a curled print appeared in ads for Velox photographic papers. It wasn't used again until the early 1940's, when it was revived to provide what the business calls "strong corporate identification." It also solved the dilemma of where to place the trademark in the ads.

Extension of the Kodak name to Eastman's textile products was decided on in 1962. Beginning that fall, it was used in ads for fabrics and garments made from the company's various polyester fibers.

Most of the history of Lea & Perrins Worcestershire Sauce is right there on the label.

John Wheeley *Lea* was a druggist in the English market town of Worcester. William *Perrins* ran a chemist shop in the nearby town of Evesham. On January 1, 1823, they organized *Lee & Perrins,* a Worcester chemist shop that was also a distribution center for pharmaceuticals, toiletries and food products concocted on the premises.

*From a recipe of a nobleman in the county* (inscribed on either side of the shield) refers to Lord Sandys, native of Worcester, ex-governor of the Indian state of Bengal and a connoisseur of exotic eastern sauces and spices. In 1835 Lord Sandys returned from Bengal with a recipe for what became the first *Worcestershire Sauce*—hence those words *the original* to distinguish it from the multitude of imitators.

*Worcestershire* translates to "county of Worcester," and the shield emblazoned on the label is the ancient coat of arms of the county.

Lord Sandys's recipe, calling for tamarinds, garlic,

eschalots, onions and molasses, almost turned out to be a catastrophe. The initial batch was unpalatable. Lord Sandys rejected it, and crocks of the stuff sat unused in Lea & Perrin's basement, where, like old wine, it mellowed.

Sometime later someone had the temerity to try another lick. It was delicious. How long did the mixture age? The company isn't telling.

The recipe, too, is top-secret and has never changed. Neither has the shape of the bottle or its wrapping. The company did consider a new design a few years ago, but rejected all proposals. After all, why change something that's been a best-seller for 136 years?

**LEVI'S**

There are two things to note about Levi's. First, they are one item of man's apparel whose basic design hasn't changed in over 100 years. Second, they get their identity not from the last name of the inventor, but from his first name.

He was Levi Strauss, an adventurous easterner who headed West by boat during the California gold rush. He struck gold all right, but not the way he expected. His fortune came from a pair of work pants, and from that day to this they've enjoyed great market success.

Young Levi got off the ship with a grubstake of tough heavy canvas fabrics, which he proposed to sell for tents and covers on Conestoga wagons—both indispensable items for the multitude of gold-seekers. When he told a miner what he had for sale the response was: "Should have brought pants."

"Pants? Why pants?" asked Levi.

"Pants don't wear worth a hoot up in the diggings. Can't get a pair strong enough to last no time."

That, at any rate, is how the makers of Levi's tell the yarn.

Levi took a few yards of his tough fabric and had them made into a pair of work pants. The miner allegedly strutted all over San Francisco proclaiming, "Look at these pants of Levi's. Doggone if a man ever had pants as strong as these before."

Over 400,000,000 pairs of the snug, low-cut pants of indigo denim have been sold since then. Cowboys, construction workers, lumbermen, farmers, miners, factory workers and suburbanites are prime customers. Ladies now have their own Levi's. ("The gals know they look right cute in these Levi's," drawls the ad copy).

But Levi's real popularity these days is among high school and college kids. For them, Levi Strauss's 120-year-old pants are exactly what the now scene calls for.

# LIFE SAVERS

Originally, they were called "Crane's Peppermint Life Savers . . . 5c . . . For That Stormy Breath." The man who created them was Clarence Crane, a small candy manufacturer in Cleveland. He introduced them as a summer item to compensate for the lagging chocolate business during the hot-weather months. Crane gave Life Savers their flavor, shape and name, and he also adapted a pharmaceutical manufacturer's pill machine to turn out "the candy mint with the hole."

But Crane could not take credit for the emergence of his creation as the most popular and profitable candy item of all time. The man to credit is Edward J. Noble, a young New York car-card salesman who tasted a Life Saver one day in 1913 and promptly struck out for Cleveland to sell car-card advertising to Crane. Instead, Noble bought Crane's Life Saver business for $2,900, $1,500 of which was supplied by Roy Allen, a friend. (Thirteen years later, Allen sold out for $3,300,000— his original investment had increased 2,200 times!)

Noble had to hustle to uncover new customers. He found them in saloons, cigar stores, barber shops, restaurants and drugstores, most of which had never sold candy. "Put Life Savers near the cash register," he pleaded. "Then be sure every customer gets a nickel with his change and see what happens."

Within a couple of years Noble was making a quarter of a million dollars annually, and by 1943 he had done so well that he was able to buy the American Broadcasting Company for $8,000,000 cash. Today, over one billion packages of Life Savers are sold annually through more than 1,000,000 outlets.

As for that hole in the middle, the company patented it years ago. It's the only patented design that can be described as: Nothing enclosed by a circle.

A Kentucky farm boy's fascination with coffee and the offhand comment of a President of the United States led to Maxwell House's "Good to the Last Drop" trademark. Joel Cheek was the farm boy. In 1873, at the age of 21, the young man left his Burkesville, Kentucky home and headed south to Nashville to seek his fortune. The young man did well as a traveling salesman for a wholesale grocery firm, but his heart wasn't in it. What he really wanted was to settle down in one spot and create an original coffee blend.

He quit his business affiliation and within a year was peddling his own coffee in the area. Among his clients was the plush Maxwell House of Nashville, which catered to everybody from itinerant musicians to European nobility. Success was assured when the hotel's guests responded enthusiastically to the dining room's new brew. Cheek was quick to dub his blend "Maxwell House Coffee."

"Good to the Last Drop," tacked on years later, was literally taken out of the mouth of Theodore Roosevelt. The story is that Roosevelt first tasted the coffee when he was a guest at the Hermitage, Andrew Jackson's old home in Nashville. Asked if he wanted a second cup, Roosevelt exclaimed: "Will I have another? Delighted! It's good to the last drop!"

Joel Cheek prospered, first as Joel Cheek & Sons, later as a partner in Cheek-Neal Company. In 1928 Maxwell House was sold for a multimillion-dollar sum to General Foods. The blend has been changed from time to time, but the priceless trademark—the tilted cup and the catchy slogan—remains the same.

## METROPOLITAN'S TOWER

It's a real tower, and it stands at One Madison Avenue in New York. For over half a century its red and white lights have been a landmark for Manhattan's millions, for residents of outlying suburbs, and for the sailors at sea. Architects Pierre and Michel Le Brun designed it, using as their pattern the famous *campanile* (or bell tower)) of St. Mark's in Venice. In 1909, when it was finished, the tower identified the 50-story Metropolitan Life Insurance building as the tallest in the world, a distinction it kept for only four years.

The adoption of the tower as a trademark came almost immediately after it was finished. Haley Fiske, a company vice-president, delivered a rousing talk at a Metropolitan convention the year the tower was completed. "The company," he declaimed, "is the light that never fails."

Merging slogan with tower symbol followed. The picture of the tower and its catchword slogan began appearing in Metropolitan ads and insurance policies.

During the First World War the light atop the building was dimmed as an electrical current-conservation measure. And on April 28, 1942, it was doused completely for three years and ten days on orders of the Eastern Defense Command, which feared the beacon could become a sighting for prowling German submarines.

Except for these two interludes, the tower, with its 144 red and white flashing bulbs and its booming Cambridge chimes signaling the hours, has faithfully performed its duty of providing a symbol of strength for the company and its policyholders.

Scholars of Greek mythology know Pegasus as the winged horse that sprang from the blood-stained earth when Medusa's head was cut off by Perseus. Motorists on America's highways are more likely to identify the Flying Red Horse as a convenient reminder to stop and fill 'er up.

That's precisely as Socony Mobil Oil Company, Inc., planned it. The winged horse is the identifying symbol of the three-billion-dollar Mobil complex of refineries, bulk plants, trucks and gas stations. It's supposed to connote great power and swiftness—just what drivers want from a gasoline.

The trademark was originally an export item. As far back as 1911, it was used by foreign subsidiaries of both Standard Oil of New York (Socony) and the Vacuum Oil Company. Its entry into the U. S. market came 22 years later, two years after organization of Socony Vacuum (now called Socony Mobil Oil Company, Inc.).

For a long time, the trademark appeared as the dominant element on the 6-foot-square Mobilgas shield on Socony Vacuum's gas stations. But back in the 1950's the company surveyed its customers to determine how many actually associated the Flying Red Horse with Mobilgas. The results were distressing. People knew the horse meant gasoline, but they weren't always sure which brand.

There followed two years of research, designing, testing and redesigning. Should the horse be dropped? Should the shield be retained? Was the word Mobilgas the right word? What about color and shape of the trademark? Researchers even devised a mathematical formula to weigh and compare all these factors.

The present sign displayed at innumerable gas stations is readable from a greater distance than the old shield. Mobil replaced Mobilgas. And blue is now the dominant color because the researchers said it has more eye appeal than red. The Flying Red Horse, however, still prances in its time-honored color.

## MORTON SALT

The admen who dreamed up the umbrella gal for the Morton Salt Company originally didn't think much of her. The year was 1914, and Morton, with about 50 years of profitable growth behind it, was preparing to advertise its new free-flowing salt. An agency was hired and a series of 12 ads scheduled. The 12 preferred drafts were shown to the company head, Sterling Morton (son of founder Joy Morton), and then one of the agency officials remembered that three other "roughs" had been brought along as extras. He presented those, too.

In Morton's own words: "I was immediately struck with one. It showed a little girl with an umbrella over her head, rain falling, a package of salt under her arm, tilted backward with spout open and salt running out. Perhaps the fact that my daughter Suzette was occupying a lot of my time and attention at that period had something to do with my interest!

"But, anyhow, it struck me that here was the whole story in a picture—that the message that the salt would

117

run in damp weather was made beautifully evident."

The slogan "When it rains, it pours" was adopted at the same time but was not copyrighted until 19 years ago, after the courts ruled slogans could be registered. As for the umbrella girl, she has gone through quite a metamorphosis over the years—from a curly-haired blonde to a straight-haired brunet and then, finally, to the current gay blonde with braids.

Seventy years is a ripe age for any trademark, but the people at the National Biscuit Company boast that their 70-year-old symbol traces its line to prehistoric times. Practically at the dawn of civilization the circle and the two bars symbolized the creation of life. The early Christians used the same symbol to demonstrate the triumph of spiritual over worldly things.

The first chairman of the cracker and cookie corporation, A. W. Green, adopted the ancient symbol as a trademark after National Biscuit was launched in 1898. A bibliophile by avocation, he came across it in an old book depicting this fifteenth-century colophon (a device placed at the end of a book or manuscript) of the Society of Printers in Venice.

Initially, the words "In-Er-Seal" appeared in the circle, exploiting the wax-paper-lined container originated by an associate of Green's. In 1918 the letters NBC were substituted, and five years later "Uneeda" was added below the seal. It has outlived such imitations as "Iwanta," "Uwanta," "Ulika" and "Abetta."

Uneeda was dropped from the trademark in 1935. Then, six years later, NBC was dropped in favor of the corporate contraction, Nabisco.

The trademark's present form usually shows the symbol in a red triangle. This dates from 1952 and was designed deliberately to draw supermarket customers' eyes to Nabisco products. Who in the fifteenth-century Venetian Society of Printers could have dreamed that such would be the destiny of the mystic colophon?

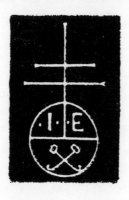

## OLYMPIC SYMBOL

Mankind's dream of a united world is graphically captured by the five rings of the Olympic flag. The five interlocked rings are a one-world symbol of the five major continents—an image of the world's peoples marching arm-in-arm. The colors of the rings (blue, yellow, black, green and red on a white field) are the colors found in the flags of most nations. In the Olympic banner, the blue is nearest the staff, the yellow links the blue and the black, the green links the black and the red.

Baron Pierre de Coubertin, a sports-minded Frenchman, created the flag in 1913, which was 2,689 years after the first Olympic race was run. The Ancient Games, begun in 776 B.C., continued for almost 1,200 years until 393 A.D., when the Roman emperor Theodosius abolished them. They were resumed in their present version in 1896, mainly because of the dedication of Baron Coubertin, who almost single-handedly persuaded an international congress of amateur sports representatives that the Olympic games should be revived.

The Baron became the sole director of the Games.

He wrote the Olympic charter and protocol and composed the athlete's oath. When he got the idea for the flag, he had the Bon Marche department store in Paris make it up to his specifications (3 meters long by 2 meters wide, with the emblem of rings measuring 2.06 meters by 60 centimeters).

The flag made its official debut in 1914 in Paris on the eighteenth anniversary of the reopening of the Olympic games. It is now kept in Lausanne, under the zealous protection of the Comité International Olympique. It flew again at the 1968 summer Olympics in Mexico City. Beneath the five hooked rings was the Olympic slogan: "CITIUS-ALTIUS-FORTIUS"—encouraging the competing athletes to efforts that are "swifter, higher, stronger."

## OSCAR

The scene: a Hollywood music hall. Time: an evening in April. The cast: Hollywood royalty and associated peerage. The action: the annual awarding-of-the-Oscars ritual.

That's the bare-boned scenario, annually played out before a global audience of TV's waiting millions. The star of the show: Oscar himself, a 13½-inch gold-plated pygmy weighing 8 pounds, the king of show business—and a copyrighted trademark.

Who is Oscar? He was born at a Hollywood banquet on May 11, 1927, a week after the Academy of Motion Picture Arts and Sciences was organized. Speaker Louis B. Mayer urged the academy to create an award for merit for the film industry. MGM art director Cedric Gibbons was in the audience and quickly sketched a figure of a "stalwart" man gripping a crusader's sword and perched on a film can. The finished art was executed by 24-year-old sculptor George Stanley.

The first "award of the statuette" was May 16, 1929.

Fifteen academy awards were bestowed, including one each to Janet Gaynor, Emil Jannings and the movie *Wings*.

The statuette might have remained nameless if a young librarian from Spokane, Mrs. Margaret Herrick, had not decided to accept a job as academy librarian in 1931. First day on the job she spotted the figure on a colleague's desk. In a burst of recognition she exclaimed, "Why, it looks just like my Uncle Oscar!" Hollywood columnist Sidney Skolsky ran the story in his feature, and "Oscar" became a household word.

Mrs. Herrick became executive director of the academy in 1943 and, until recent retirement, was the person who firmly administered all academy activities, including bestowal of the Oscars that she had named.

Over 1,200 replicas of the gold-plated symbol have been awarded. The champion recipient was Walt Disney, who won 30. The most-Oscared actor is Walter Brennan (three), the most-Oscared actress, Katherine Hepburn (three).

Oscar, incidentally, cannot be sold on the open market. Only the academy can buy it back—for $10. His gold plate is a cover-up for the interior of $92\frac{1}{2}\%$ tin and $7\frac{1}{2}\%$ copper. But to any of filmdom's people, the value of this tin god is hardly measurable.

Any day now some smart press agent may leak out the news that Liz Taylor—Hollywood's best-known Cleopatra—anoints herself with the same olive and palm oils as the original Cleopatra, and any feminine admirer can emulate her with a dime bar of soap available in drugstores and supermarkets.

The soap, obviously, is Palmolive, and the tie-in with Cleopatra goes back half a century to an advertising campaign keyed to the theme that the secret of Cleopatra's charms was olive and palm oils in her bath—the same oils used in Palmolive soap. To women of the day, it was an irresistible pitch.

Palmolive's success probably was as big a surprise to its originator as anyone. He was W. B. Johnson, a young chemist just out of college, who worked for his father's soap company. He perfected the soap in the late 1890's and gave it its name.

By 1910, Palmolive was doing well, but not well enough. A chance meeting with Claude Hopkins, one of advertising's greats, gave Johnson the opening he needed. The company was renamed The Palmolive Company. Coupon deals were devised. The firm became a pioneer in selling soap in groceries as well as drugstores. And a famous slogan was coined: "Keep that schoolgirl complexion." It had more wholesome overtones than the Cleopatra pitch.

Palmolive became the world's biggest-selling toilet soap. In 1926, the company merged with Peet Bros., another soap firm; two years later came a major coup: merger with the ailing Colgate & Company, then in its second century.

The Palmolive people have tried to profit from their product's relationship to Cleopatra. A few years ago they introduced a new brand, called "Cleopatra," but it wasn't that authentic. Unlike Palmolive soap, it contained neither the palm nor the olive oils that delicately scented the bath of the original Cleo.

Hollywood rarely does things in nonspectacular fashion. Stars are never brighter, mountains never higher, a man's vision never broader than in the soaring imaginations of the movie moguls. Thus moviedom's trademarks are neither subtle nor modest, as is evidenced by Paramount's mountains superimposed on clouds and encircled by 24 stars.

It is a grand concept, adopted primarily because one man, Adolph Zukor, liked it. Zukor, who started out as a proprietor of a New York penny arcade, helped to build one of Hollywood's major film companies.

In 1912, shortly after he imported Sarah Bernhardt's "Queen Elizabeth" as the first full-length movie shown in the U.S., Zukor founded Famous Players Company to make films in New York. At about the same time, four Hollywood showmen—Jesse L. Lasky, Cecil B. De Mille, Dustin Farnum and Samuel Goldwyn—founded the Jesse L. Lasky Feature Play Company, and William W. Hodkinson organized a film distribution firm called Paramount Pictures. Zukor agreed to supply half of the films Hodkinson planned to distribute.

Lasky merged with Zukor four years later, and the

combination purchased Paramount to form Famous Players-Lasky Corporation. Their major asset: an actress named Mary Pickford. The name subsequently became Paramount-Famous-Lasky Corporation, then Paramount Publix, then Paramount Pictures, Inc., and, in 1950, Paramount Pictures Corporation. At the present time Paramount is a Gulf-Western property.

Former penny arcadian Adolph Zukor, the first head of Paramount, chose the trademark. An artist in the company's art department, Vincent Trotta, gets credit for the design. He tried his hand at it after Zukor rejected all the entries submitted by top artists commissioned to create a suitable symbol for Paramount. Zukor liked Trotta's design, and moviegoers have been seeing it on the screen ever since.

## MR. PEANUT

For a fellow who is crowding 60 Mr. Peanut is a remarkably spry specimen, saucy, with a flair all his own. A legal ruling once referred to the trademark as "a dude—a spindly-legged creature, top-hatted, spatted and monocled, carrying a cane." His creator and sponsor (Planters Peanuts) wouldn't change him for all the peanuts in Georgia.

A schoolboy—now forgotten—dreamed up the animated peanut. A commercial artist added cane, hat and monocle. An Italian-born former fruit-stand operator of Wilkes-Barre, Pennsylvania, named Amedeo Obici, was the moving force behind the whole project and also the founder of what is today a multimillion-dollar business. Obici, together with a friend as a partner, elevated the peanut from its turn-of-the-century status of "monkey food" to its present respectability.

They pioneered packaging peanuts in glassine and cellophane packages and vacuum-packed cans. They also were shrewd and resourceful merchandisers and promoters. Their master stroke was sponsoring the contest that brought Mr. Peanut into being in 1916. For it was the schoolboy's sketch sent in as a contest entry that was developed into a priceless property for the firm.

Riding the trademark's invisible coattails to fame has been that word "Planters," which, it turns out, means absolutely nothing. Obici picked it when the company was organized in 1906 because it sounded "important and dignified."

In its day a powerful ad line was the company's now-abandoned slogan, "The Nickel Lunch." It helped make peanuts a national snack.

The property of Standard Brands, Inc., since 1960, Mr. Peanut has marched in parades, walked down the nation's Main Streets and the Atlantic City boardwalk, been reproduced in toys, souvenirs and pocket gadgets, memorialized in statues, lighted up in a mammoth Broadway spectacular sign, used as a premium and exploited in just about every way imaginable. The payoff? In his 55 years of existence, selling candy, nuts and peanut butter, Mr. Peanut's total take has been in the area of a billion dollars.

## PHILIP MORRIS'S JOHNNY

Back when people thought that all smoking might do to you was stunt your growth, Philip Morris hired a 50-inch-high pitchman for its product—thus demonstrating its indifference to this particular indictment against the cigaret habit. The midget was a former bellhop from Brooklyn named Johnny Roventini. For over 30 years Johnny has helped Philip Morris stand high in the race for cigaret customers.

The actual trademark preceded Johnny by about ten years and depicted a snappy-looking bellboy with his "Call for Philip Morris." The name of the symbol's creator is lost in the company's lore. But well-recorded is the story of how Milton Biow, head of the company's ad department, set out on a deliberate hunt for a live Johnny and found him in the lobby of the New Yorker hotel.

It was 1933 and radio advertising was opening new vistas to promotion and selling. Johnny's perfect B-flat vocal cords blended nicely with the dominant E-flat of "On the Trail" from Ferde Grofé's "Grand Canyon Suite." Many of today's middle-aged Americans remember well that first program of "Johnny presents . . . ," featuring Grofé himself and the haunting "On the Trail" theme behind Johnny's urgent "Call for Phil-lip Mor-ress."

Johnny Roventini was a hit. In the 1930's and 1940's, Johnny "presented" such name bands as Harry James, Leo Reisman, Ray Block and Johnny Green. He made guest appearances on such top radio shows of the pre-TV era as "This Is Your Life," "The Rudy Vallee Show" and "Break the Bank."

Johnny also developed into a great handshaker for his employers. In the course of his public appearances he has shaken over a million hands.

This is one of those trademarks about which a number of stories—all of them false—have been told. Even some Phillips Petroleum Company employes don't know how the company symbol evolved. These were some of the reasons they gave when asked about the trademark's origin:

• Frank Phillips was 66 years old when he organized the company. (He was actually 44.)

• The 66 referred to 66 octane. (Octane ratings weren't adopted until five years after the name was chosen.)

• The company's first refinery was won in a crap game from an owner who rolled double sixes. (This is a confusion with the 6666 Ranch, which, according to legend, changed hands in a Texas-size poker game. The winning hand was four sixes.)

• The 66 was chosen because there are 66 books in the Bible. (False.)

• The company basketball team won by 66 points on the night before the name was chosen. (The game was won by a score of 32 to 14.)

• The first Phillips gas station sold 6,600 gallons the first day. (It sold 12,000 gallons.)

So what are the facts? In November 1927, the com-

pany had everything ready to market its gasoline—
except the name. The gasoline's fuel gravity was close
to 66. And the company's new refinery was near U.S.
Highway 66. But suggestions to use the 66 got nowhere.

Then, on the eve of a special meeting to select a
name, a Phillips official was road-testing the new fuel.
"This car goes like sixty," he exclaimed.

"Sixty, nothing," responded the driver. "We're doing sixty-six!"

The story was repeated at the next day's meeting.
Asked where it happened, the official replied: "Near Tul-
sa, on Highway 66."

The committee decided that all the omens were good.
Phillips 66 became the official name. All of which
proves that when creating trademarks, a whim can be
as good as an exhaustive market survey.

Pillsbury's XXXX symbol was adopted in 1872, but its roots go back almost 2,000 years, to the early Christian era. Shortly after the death of Christ, millers and bakers adopted an XXX symbol for bread, each X representing one of the crosses on Calvary. Subsequently the original symbolism was lost, but medieval millers continued to use the triple-X mark as a grading symbol for top-quality flour.

In time this practice, too, died out until 1872, when miller Charles A. Pillsbury, then three years in the flour business, heard the legend and promptly adopted the symbol—but with an extra X. "If three X's mean the best, then we'll add another, just to show that Pillsbury's Best is really the best," is the way he is supposed to have put it.

The Pillsbury sacks, prominently decorated with the XXXX trademark, were strictly for flour, African aborigines and American back-country folks until 1957, when high fashion went all-out for the sack. As a result, the Pillsbury model showed up on a shapely lass featured on the "Steve Allen Show," was worn at a

Hotel Greeters of America convention, and was adapted for cotton batiste nighties fashioned by Sans Souci.

You can be sure Pillsbury was grateful to Paris for the sack fashion trend while it lasted.

## PROCTER AND GAMBLE

The moon and stars symbol may appear on more products than any other. You have to look closely to find it, but it is on a multitude of brands of detergents, soap, food and toiletries, including Tide, Cheer, Oxydol, Joy, Ivory, Comet, Camay, Mr. Clean, Dreft, Dash, Spic and Span, Crisco, Fluffo, Folger, Duncan Hines, Crest, Gleem, Downy, Head & Shoulders, Lilt, Secret, Big Top and Jif. All of them are made by Procter & Gamble, a mammoth two-and-a-half-billion-dollar enterprise, said to be the nation's biggest advertiser (over $270,000,000 a year). The trademark is P & G's corporate symbol.

It goes back to founders William Procter (a candle maker) and James Gamble (a soap maker), who established the firm in 1837 in the thriving river port of Cincinnati. Procter and Gamble were brothers-in-law, married to the daughters of a local chandler. One of the major products of the firm was "Star" candles, which packet boats delivered up and down the Ohio and Mississippi rivers.

Illiterate longshoremen would chalk a crude star on

each case of the candles for easy identification. Later the star was enclosed in a circle. Then more stars were added. For reasons now obscure, a Neptunish man-in-the-moon was added in 1859. A few years later, inspired by an old American flag he saw in a restaurant, William Procter ordered 13 stars embedded in the trademark's firmament.

Once, back when candles were a major product, company officials decided the trademark was meaningless and had to go. The outcry from customers was immediate and loud. They said candles without the symbol weren't "genuine." You can be sure the proposal was never repeated. The trademark has stayed, even though the company long ago dropped its line of candles.

The Rock of Gibraltar, the Prudential Insurance Company's trademark, it said to have been inspired by "Snake Hill," a shelf rock that juts upward from the Jersey meadows near the New York to Newark rail line. Search for this symbol of invulnerability began in 1895, when Prudential President John F. Dryden met adman Charles Austin Bates on a voyage home from Europe. Dryden was impressed with advertising's new growth and commissioned Bates to come up with a symbol of "lasting, enduring strength" for Prudential.

Bates tried for several months, finally admitted failure. That's when Mortimer Remington, young account executive of the J. Walter Thompson agency in New York, was assigned the job and hit upon the Gibraltar idea. The story is that Remington had his brainstorm while gazing out a train window at Snake Hill on his way to the office.

Dryden lost no time in exploiting the "Rock" with the slogan "The Prudential Has the Strength of Gibraltar." *Leslie's Weekly* carried the trademark first, in its August 20, 1896, issue. From that day to this it has appeared in practically every ad and piece of literature issued by the firm, is used in TV advertising, and is inscribed on Prudential's policies.

It is one of the few trademarks that had ready-made international recognition. Is there a schoolboy in the world who doesn't recognize the "Rock" when he sees it?

The origin of some trademarks is obscured in the uncertainties of history, and the Quaker Oats Man is one of these. When you attempt to pin-point the name of the man who chose it, you come upon a conflict. It's generally agreed that credit should go to one of two partners, Henry D. Seymour or William Heston. These two, along with two others, organized a small oatmeal milling company in the 1870's at Ravenna, Ohio, hoping to profit from the new but growing oatmeal business. The enterprise was short-lived. Within two years, it was sold and aside from its Quaker trademark, contributed an insignificant chapter to the history of to-day's giant Quaker Oats Company.

Seymour's version of the trademark's genesis was that he searched an encyclopedia for ideas and hit upon Quaker because "the purity of the lives of the people, their sterling honesty, their strength and manliness" impressed him.

In Heston's version, Heston came upon a picture of William Penn one day while walking through the streets of Cincinnati. Being of Quaker ancestry, he is said to have been struck by Penn's garb and character as connoting just the qualities he was looking for.

The Quaker trademark endured and became an indispensable asset of successor companies as the years wore on. It has been the subject of costly lawsuits here and abroad. In 1915 the Society of Friends waged an unsuccessful fight in Congress to bar all trademarks bearing the name of religious denominations.

The transition of the Quaker Oats Man from the 1870's to the Quaker Oats Man of today has been startling. Originally a little man garbed in dark and drab garments, he has emerged as a genial, ruddy-cheeked, expansive fellow.

## RALSTON'S CHECKERBOARD

Ralston Purina's nine-square checkerboard had its genesis in a nostalgic memory of the company founder, William H. Danforth. As a boy, young Bill swept the floor, stocked the shelves and served the customers in his dad's country store in Charleston, Missouri. Frugal farm housewives of the period would buy bargain-priced bolts of cloth when it came time to outfit the family in shirts and dresses, resulting in instant recognition of all the progeny who were wearing the same stripes, checks, or other patterns. One family would show up on a Saturday morning clad in red and white checks, and the visual impact was unforgettable.

Years later, when Danforth launched his Purina Chows product line, he recalled those red checks. He reasoned that if he remembered that family, then a red-checkered trademark would help customers remember his chows.

No doubt the theory contributed to the company's prosperity—the checkerboard trademark is now registered in 79 countries and is carried on 558 different products in this country alone. The checkerboard pattern has become an integral part of Purina's package designs.

The square became a touchstone of some homely Danforth philosophy. "Think tall, stand tall, smile tall, live tall," he used to say, with the four-fold credo symbolized by the trademark's four-sided appearance. Another Danforth observation from the square was that it conveyed the meaning of a well-planned life, soundly developed in the four aspects of social, mental, physical and religious balance.

Homely philosophy notwithstanding, the company has made solid promotional capital out of the trademark. There aren't many firms that can claim their trademark as a mailing address, but in St. Louis, Ralston Purina is headquartered in Checkerboard Square.

One thing about that midnight ride of Paul Revere: More is known about it than about the trademark that is stamped on products of the firm he founded, Revere Copper & Brass, Incorporated. Every schoolboy can recite the details of Paul's sweep through the streets of Lexington. But today's custodians of the Revere name candidly concede there is little known about the what-where-and-why of the company's star-encircled trademark.

A couple of things, however, are clear.

• The profile is not Paul Revere's. Careful comparison with old engravings shows conclusively that Paul never looked like that.

• The symbol of Paul on a galloping horse, also used by the company, has never been a registered trademark. The star-encircled profile above, most recently redesigned in 1965, is the official company identification.

While details of the origins and inspiration of the trademark are fuzzy, the company has detailed documentation of Paul Revere's skills as a metal craftsman. "The emphasis placed on Revere's equestrian episode tends to obscure his true stature as one of the world's great craftsmen and artisans, a pioneer manufacturer and industrialist," a company official once complained. Caster of cannons and bells, a silversmith, a shipfitter, a craftsman who sheathed the roof of the Massachusetts statehouse and the hull of the *Constitution* in copper, Paul Revere set down strong roots for what is today a major metal-working firm.

Sons and grandsons of the founder have served the company and Revere descendants have sat on the board. Vague as are the origins of the patriot's profile appearing on the company trademark, it does link today's company with its illustrious founder.

In the designer's lexicon, different symbols convey different meanings. The cross is a sign of hope. The swastika connotes good luck or a Nazi horror. And something called a monad can be the symbol for the most elementary form of life—or for the second-largest supermarket chain in the country.

The chain is Safeway. The trademark, developed in 1952, is based on the monad in which the two interlocked "tear drop" forms contained in a circle have been spun into the flowing lines of a liquid-looking "S." The symbol was designed to be as visual on a box of raisins as on the side of a truck.

The story of Safeway began over half a century ago when a young homesteader named M. B. Skaggs helped his minister-father establish a store for the parishioners in American Falls, Idaho. Skaggs liked the grocery business, commuted 20 miles on horseback to run his dad's place, and tried such daring innovations as selling a freight-car load of peaches, cash-and-carry, at the train siding. It was in this tradition that the Safeway chain was later to pioneer cash-and-carry selling, self-service, produce by the pound, and disposable milk cartons.

Business was good, Skaggs was enterprising, and in a few years Skaggs United Stores was a going operation. Then the merger bug hit, and Skaggs sold out to a chain of southern California food stores in 1926. This chain had just changed its name from Seelig-Weldon Stores to Safeway—a name selected in a public competition.

Today Safeway is the number two chain in the nation's biggest industry (the food business is bigger than autos, steel and aerospace combined). It operates over 2,000 supermarkets, heavily concentrated in the West but also scattered all over the country and in a few English communities.

Safeway has demonstrated solid money-making ability in recent years. Of every dollar taken in at the average Safeway check-out counter, about 1.6 cents is figured as profit. With total business in the billions, the 1.6 per cent profit adds up to a fat sum annually. Obviously, Safeway's monad-S has proved to be a good luck symbol.

# SALADA
## TEA

"Plan for the future. That's where you'll spend the rest of your life." That bit of philosophy appears on a little tag attached to a Salada tea bag, and it couldn't have more meaning for anyone than it did for the founder of the company, Peter C. Larkin.

As a wholesale grocery salesman back in the 1880's, he planned well while he made his rounds in Canada's eastern Ontario. He observed that Ceylon tea had made a big hit in Britain but had yet to compete with the China blends sold in the U. S. and Canada. Larkin quit his job, packed Ceylon tea by hand in lead foil containers, and sealed it with a wrap-around label. He called it the "Golden Tea Pot Blend" of the Salada Ceylon Tea Company, Ltd. Hand packing was obviously too slow, so the inventive Mr. Larkin perfected semi-automatic tea packing machinery, which he sold all over the world. As for that name Salada, he had heard it once as the name of a small Indian tea garden, long since lost in history. He adopted it for his tea because he liked the sound of it and thought it would be easily remembered.

Larkin ultimately became Canadian High Commissioner to Britain. His son, Gerald R., took over the family business and finally, in 1957, sold it to Shirriff-

Horsey, which then became Salada-Shirriff-Horsey.

Adman John W. Colpitts had the inspiration for Salada's bits of folksy and humorous gleanings. It takes four or five minutes for the tea to steep, so why not give people something to ponder while they wait? Among the 496 aphorisms now in circulation are these:

"It's better to have loved a short man than never to have loved a tall."

"Chop your own wood and it will warm you twice."

"To avoid that run-down feeling, cross streets carefully."

## SAMSON CORD

Anyone who has reeved lines on a sloop or hitched cord to a window sash or hauled the ropes to recover a space capsule may recognize this trademark. The picture of Samson wrestling with the lion in his den stands for the Samson Cordage Works, manufacturers of rope. It is the nation's oldest registered trademark.

The founder of the company, New Englander James Pike Tolman, chose the trademark (issued July 4, 1884) as a symbol of brute power encountering its match. In Tolman's mind, the strength of Samson was something to be equated with the strength of his braided rope. Tolman's sister had been struck by the paintings of Samson and the lion she had seen in her tours of European art galleries and suggested adapting the biblical story as the basis for a trademark. His mother and wife are also listed in the family annals as contributors to the design.

In 1888 the Tolman Company changed its name to the Samson Cordage Works, thus making the company's name and the trademark's identity one and the same.

With a Boston tea merchant, Lucius G. Pratt, as his partner, Tolman prospered. His engineering ingenuity was responsible for the design of 13 rope-braiding machines and devices, some of them still in use.

Sash cord and clothesline were the major uses for the company's product. Then, in the 1950's, automatic dryers made clotheslines nearly obsolete and modern window designs reduced the need for sash cord.

Samson wrestled with this challenge and conquered it. It designed new ropes and found new and bigger markets in the space program and the booming boating business.

It still makes the old standbys, however, and it boasts that its Spot Cord sash cord has changed hardly at all, except for the addition of a synthetic core to add strength. One of its proudest achievements was the manufacture of a five-mile single length of rope used to dangle delicate electronic equipment above the ocean floor.

It was 33 years between the time the first shovel of dirt was turned for the building of the Santa Fe and the adoption of the railroad's trademark. Ground-breaking occurred on October 30, 1868. In 1901, tradition has it, a couple of officials were discussing the design for a trademark when one of them traced a circle with a silver dollar to symbolize wheels of transportation. Inside he placed a cross to which he assigned a triple meaning: First, it symbolized the four points of the compass; second, it was the cross carried by the Franciscan padres during the explorations of the Spanish conquistadors in the Southwest; third, it was the pagan sign of the sun used by the Indians centuries before white men set foot in the colorful lands of the Santa Fe. Thus was born one of railroading's best-known symbols.

Officially, the railroad is "The Atchison, Topeka and Santa Fe Railway Company," so the trademark is a concession to passengers, freight men, officials and railway buffs who have always called it the Santa Fe. Atchison and Topeka were outposts on the Kansas frontier when Cyrus Holliday, founder of Topeka, first had his dream of building a railroad westward across the Rockies and the desert via Santa Fe to the Pacific.

Topeka was the meeting point for two famous mule train trails—the Santa Fe and the California. Holliday chose to chart his line along the old Santa Fe trail, and not so long ago passengers on the railway's crack transcontinental fliers could see the remains of the trail as they sped across the wastelands.

A crisis simmered in the auto plants of Detroit in 1925. Almost overnight, public taste had decreed that two-tone cars were the thing, along with racoon coats and flapper hair-do's. Quick-drying lacquers and the newly invented automatic spray guns made the two-tone finishes possible. But one problem plagued the manufacturers: They were having an awful time achieving a clean, sharp edge where one color met another on the auto body.

Makeshift masking techniques, using newspapers and wrapping paper backed with homemade glue or stuck to the surface with surgical tape, were tried and discarded. Desperately needed was a masking tape that would stick tightly, seal against paint solvents, and come off easily without taking the paint with it.

Richard Drew, a laboratory employe of Minnesota Mining and Manufacturing Company ("3M"), then involved principally with abrasives, heard of the problem. His research resulted in development of a masking tape coated with a rubber based adhesive.

One edge held the masking paper in place. The other

edge adhered to the auto body surface. Economy-minded 3M figured no adhesive was needed in the middle so didn't put any there. But when the tape had its initial test in the paint shops, it failed to hold properly.

Back to the 3M salesmen went this message from the painters: "Take this tape back to those Scotch bosses of yours and tell them to put adhesive all over the tape, not just on the edges."

Thus was born the moniker "Scotch brand tape" and, to coin an obvious pun, the name stuck.

Since then 3M has prospered and grown, and today its line of pressure-sensitive tapes includes more than 300 different types.

A few years back the company boasted that if all the tapes produced by 3M that year were stretched end to end, there would be enough to reach the moon and back seven times. Quite a space-age achievement for a firm whose bosses were once accused of being "Scotch."

## SHERWIN-WILLIAMS PAINTS

This symbol was conceded to be more than a modest exaggeration when the Sherwin-Williams Company adopted it as its trademark in 1905. The company did little exporting in those days, so when the trademark was proposed, founding president Henry Sherwin wondered about the validity of the symbol even though he was taken with the idea.

Walter H. Cottingham, Sherwin's general manager and a live-wire promoter, put Sherwin's reservations to rest with the exhortation: "Let's adopt this Cover-the-Earth trademark and make it come true!" That's exactly what happened. The firm's global business now more than justifies the trademark.

George W. Ford, for many years ad manager of the company, sketched the original in 1895, but laid it aside, possibly because he didn't want to tread on boss Sherwin's toes; the trademark then was a chameleon mounted on a painter's palette, the brainchild of you-guess-who.

Three years later (1898) Ford unearthed his sketch, the boss liked it, and by 1905 the chameleon was in limbo as the company's official trademark. Cover-the-Earth is undoubtedly worth millions, but is carried on the company's books at only $1.

Study the trademark carefully and you'll note that the world is askew, with its axis almost horizontal instead of vertical. Reason: The company wanted its paint flowing not from the North Pole but from Cleveland, Ohio, headquarters of Sherwin-Williams.

"Mellow" is a word often applied to cigarets and beer but rarely to crude oil and certainly never to dinosaurs. But when Sinclair Refining Company began to use a picture of a brontosauras (order Sauropoda) in its advertising 39 years ago, it was "to dramatize the age and mellowness" of the crude oil that Sinclair refined.

The idea caught on fast. The company drew attention with its exhibit of a life-size dinosaur model at the Chicago Century of Progress Exposition in 1933-34, and, two years later, at the Dallas World's Fair.

Dinosaur bones were the object of American Museum of Natural History expeditions into the Rockies and Texas sponsored by Sinclair.

In the mid-thirties, the company issued its initial Dinosaur Stamp Album, of which 4,000,000 were printed along with 96,000,000 stamps. Children of the thirties who are now parents request copies for their children.

The decision to adopt the dinosaur as the company's official trademark came 12 years ago. Simultaneously, the company stopped using the circular "H-C" (for high compression) signs on its service stations.

The new sign, with red lettering and green dinosaur, is used in all the company's activities. A major step was adoption of the name "Dino" for Sinclair's regular gasoline. A big crisis occurred with the question of how to depict the 67-foot dinosaur in a TV commercial. A three-foot model, complete with moving legs, head and tail, was designed and, thanks to the magic of the TV camera, performed admirably.

The Smith Brothers were real people whose century-old nicknames, "Trade" and "Mark," evolved as a result of competition in the cough drop trade and a printer's whimsy. "Trade" was William Smith and "Mark" was Andrew Smith, both sons of James Smith, an itinerant carpenter who migrated from St. Armand, Quebec, to the Hudson River town of Poughkeepsie, New York in 1847. Papa Smith gave up carpentry to open a restaurant; one day a customer offered Smith a "secret" formula for a cough candy. Smith stirred up batches of the stuff on the kitchen stove and advertised the "drops" as a remedy for all "afflicted with hoarseness, coughs or colds."

Young William and Andrew took over on their father's death in 1866. They set up a small plant in a loft and sold the drops to stores up and down the valley. Success bred imitators ("Schmitt Brothers," "Smythe Sisters," plus other "Smith Brothers"), and it was then that an identifying trademark for the original became urgent. What better identity than a picture of the two bearded brothers?

It first went on small envelopes, then on factory-filled packages, always with "Trade" under William, "Mark" under Andrew.

By the late nineteenth century, the genuine Smith Brothers Cough Drops were a commercial success, with daily output measured in the tons. The line has been expanded to include Smith Brothers Menthol Cough Drops (1922), a Cough Syrup (1926), Wild Cherry Cough Drops (1948) and Assorted Fruit Cough Drops and Smokers Drops (both 1958).

Chairman of the board today is fourth-generation Robert Smith, great-grandson of James, who boasts not a beard but a moustache.

For 64 years Squibb got along with the trademark on the left. Classic in design, positive in its meaning, it put across the message of what the Squibb name stood for. Then a few years ago the old trademark was shelved and in its place came the new one on the right. Why this change?

Says Squibb: The new trademark is "more defined and modern." It expresses "strength, exactness and dependability." It is "new, more contemporary," "impressive and precise" and obviously makes Squibb "a more prominent part of the trademark." A spokesman adds: The new mark has the practical advantage of being "cleaner, crisper and easier to decipher than the old one."

The pharmaceutical company, founded by Dr. Edward Robinson Squibb in 1858, didn't have a trademark until 1905, when the Greek-columned symbol was designed by some nameless artist. Column No. 3 originally read "efficiency," but "efficacy" replaced it in 1920 on grounds that the word more accurately conveyed the company's pride in its quality control. The only other change, prior to the recent radical streamlining, came in 1961 when "research" was inserted in the base of the columns, a counterpoint to "reliability" on the capstone.

The new design retains a suggestion of Greek columns, providing continuity with the previous version.

It also has another advantage: The company's seal has long been used on products sold to Spanish, French, Portuguese, Italian, Turkish and Japanese markets. The new seal gets around the problem of multiple translations by giving the company a universal—and almost wordless—trademark for its global operations.

# PLEASE!

## ONLY YOU CAN
## PREVENT FOREST FIRES

## SMOKEY THE BEAR

This is a yarn that begins in the dark days after Pearl Harbor and ends happily in a cozy little enclave of the Washington zoo.

In 1942 the Goleta oil field, just north of Santa Barbara in California, was shelled by a Japanese submarine. Reaction was swift. Among other defense measures, the U.S. Forest Service and the National Association of State Foresters moved to prevent saboteurs or anyone else from igniting the tinder-dry forest along the Pacific Coast. They went to the public with a plea for help, using posters, publicity and ads contributed by the Advertising Council, Inc., to convey the message.

Walt Disney offered the services of Bambi the deer as a poster personality, but in 1945 Bambi was succeeded by a bear in trousers and ranger hat, drawn by commercial artist Albert Staehle and promptly dubbed Smokey.

War over, the menace of forest fires was still very much a concern. Smokey acquired permanent status, and today the fire-prevention campaign is an impressive success, utilizing posters, comic books, ads, radio and TV programs (in which Smokey talks), calendars and stamps. The Junior Forest Ranger Program has enlisted 4,000,000 boys and girls to help Smokey Bear prevent forest fires. Between 3,000 and 4,000 new members join the club each week. They get a badge, membership card, bookmark, Smokey's song and a letter from Smokey. All of this promotion has reduced man-caused forest fires by almost half and has cut destroyed acreage by 80%.

Yes, there is a real Smokey. He was a cub picked up in 1950 more dead than alive after a forest fire in the Lincoln National Forest in New Mexico. He now lives in the Washington Zoo, probably the most indulged bruin in history. He has a wife, Goldie, but thus far no little Smokies.

State Farm Insurance Company thinks it paid twice
for its trademark of three interlocking ovals. Once to
Mrs. Marjorie King of Knoxville, Illinois, an ex-employee who vaguely recalls suggesting the design back
in the 30's. She got $2 for it. The second time was to
W. J. M. Allcock of Elm Grove, West Virginia, also
an ex-employee. He got $10 and a commendation.

Whoever was the originator, State Farm is well aware
of what a bargain it got. The three-oval design symbolizes the company's expansion from auto insurance to
life insurance and then to fire, theft and general insurance.

State Farm was founded in 1922 by an Illinois
farmer, George J. Mecherle, who decided farmers would
support a mutual insurance company. He realized that
the future of farm transportation was the automobile,
not the horse. For years the company has been a leader
in the auto insurance business and today has millions
of policyholders.

Farmer Mecherle planted the seed of the trademark
with his first company emblem. It was an oval enclosing
a car, vintage 1922. On the outer border were the

words "State Farm Mutual Auto Ins. Co., Bloomington, Illinois." Inside with the car were the words "Service, Satisfaction, Safety, Economy." Five years later the life insurance company was founded. Its emblem: an oval enclosing a cornucopia with the words "Plenty for You and Yours." In 1935 came the fire insurance company and another oval, this time enclosing a fireman's hat with the word "Fire."

Hooking the three together—by either Mrs. King or Mr. Allcock—came naturally, but the company dallied for almost 20 years (until 1955) before it finally got around to registering the trademark.

# Sunbeam

Well-established as it is, the Sunbeam trademark can be traced back only so far, after which its origins become cloudy. What is known is that it was adopted in 1921 and was initially used as a trade name for electric flatirons. What is not known is who chose it as a trademark, or why the word "sunbeam" was hit upon by its originators. One guess is that the word conveyed the picture of clean-smelling laundry, dried in the sun, and finished with an iron that would preserve this sun-dried freshness.

The flatiron, originally called "Princess," was made by the Chicago Flexible Shaft Company. This firm got its start in 1897, producing hand-powered shearing machines for farmers. It also achieved some fame for its production of industrial furnaces and for Clark Heater, named for one of the founding partners, and used as a foot warmer in horse-drawn carriages during the early years of the century.

The switch to household-type products began with the flatiron and the Rain King sprinkler. A major coup was the Mixmaster, introduced in 1930 and claimed to be the first of its type. Later came coffee makers, electric shavers, waffle bakers, toasters, electric clocks, vacuum cleaners, floor conditioners, power mowers, plus a great variety of other products. Other "firsts" claimed by the firm include the electric frying pan (1953), woman's electric shaver (1955) and the cap-type hair dryer (1956).

By 1946 it was clear the firm needed an all-embracing trademark, and "Sunbeam," which had already brought national recognition to a few of the company's products, was selected. Today, everything the company makes—from animal clippers to kitchen blenders—carries the Sunbeam label.

Legendary as are its origins, the trademark isn't totally without meaning. A few years back, a company official tinkered with it, striving to convert it to a meaningful descriptive. He succeeded—but only partially. From the second syllable ("beam") he evolved the company's slogan: "Best Electric Appliances Made."

## SUN-MAID

The specifications were simple enough when the California Associated Raisin Company launched its search for an eye-catching brand name and trademark. All it wanted, it said, was something that indicated the raisins were sun-dried, not artificially dried. Almost as an afterthought, the cooperative of raisin producers specified that the trademark should include a pretty girl.

First came the conversion of the words "sundried" into "sun-made." Then the sunbonnet girl was created, carrying her tray dripping with luscious raisin grapes. After that, the designers did the obvious—they changed "sun-made" to "Sun-Maid," and a trademark was born. The girl in the sunbonnet was no artist's dream. She was Lorraine Collett, an employee of the cooperative.

All this took place in 1911 and except for an occasional modernization, the symbol of girl, grapes and tray against the backdrop of a sunburst has remained unchanged. In fact, the trademark was so successful the organization decided to change its name to Sun-Maid Raisin Growers of California.

The raisin growers are well-satisfied with their choice. They say it's a rare housewife who doesn't know what the trademark identifies when she sees it. The smiling face beneath the sunbonnet has become internationally famous and is well-known in most of Europe, the Orient and in the farthest reaches of South America —where the Spanish version of Sun-Maid is "La Hija del Sol," daughter of the sun.

Yes, there was a girl named Tootsie. She was an Austrian "Wiener Madchen"—a pretty young thing from Vienna—who was the childhood sweetheart of Leo Hirshfield. And everybody called her "Tootsie."

Leo Hirshfield was a candymaker. He also was a young man of ambition and, in the parlance of the day, he "left his native home to seek brighter horizons in the land of opportunity"—which, of course, was the U.S.A. In 1896 Leo found his way to New York City, where he settled down in a combined store and apartment. He had brought with him one valuable asset: the formula for a chewy, chocolaty candy that he made in roll form and sold for a penny a piece. This, he decided, was his key to riches—if only he could find a catchy name for it.

That's when Hirshfield gave his sweetheart a sort of immortality at the candy counter. He called his product "Tootsie Roll" and proceeded to sell it in his candy shop. It was an immediate hit with youngsters, the story goes, and production has soared from 200 rolls a day to millions. Today the four factories of Tootsie Roll Industries, Inc., (two of them in Mexico City and Barcelona) strain to keep up with the demand.

What does "Tootsie" mean? It must have been a very special name for a very special girl. The Austrian embassy in Washington disclaims all knowledge of it. The embassy says there are similar terms of endearment: "Putzi," "Kutzi"—but "Tutzi"? "Ach, nein!"

# THE TRAVELERS

Businessman, architect, scholar, entrepreneur, Connecticut Yankee James G. Batterson was always on the lookout for a good idea and he found one in England during a visit around 1860. It was travel insurance, sold to passengers on the English railroad. When Batterson arrived back home in Connecticut, he organized an insurance company to protect people "journeying by railway or steamboat." The name: Travelers Insurance Company. Its symbol: an umbrella to represent what it sold—"protection."

The umbrella became part of the company's promotion package, along with other gimmicks — free pocket calendars, paperweights, war maps, election return scorecards. One official, the first manager of the New York office, sensed the dramatic possibilities of the symbol early in the 1900's. He gave coachmen and truckmen big oversized cotton umbrellas with the words "Insure in Travelers" emblazoned all over them. But full exploitation of the umbrella was yet to come.

The company grew to become the twenty-fifth largest corporation in the country, and traveler's insurance became a very small item in the firm's total line of life, accident, health, auto and other types of protection. The multibillion-dollar enterprise decided to intensify its use of the umbrella. Today the red symbol with the white-circled T gets fantastic exposure: stationery, ads, earrings, golf balls, even lollipops. About 75,000 umbrellas go to clients every year. At least one of these ended up in Russia when a seaman (a Travelers man on reserve duty) traded with a Russian scientist on an adjoining oceanographic ship in Bermuda. The seaman got a Sputnik medal. The Soviet scientist got a very red Travelers umbrella.

# Upjohn

Young Dr. William Erastus Upjohn had made a promising start in Kalamazoo. His practice was good and his prospects bright. But he had enough time on his hands to experiment in his laboratory, focusing on development of a friable (easily crumbled) pill.

The experiment was successful. The pill was patented, and he and his brother, Dr. Henry Upjohn, organized the Upjohn Pill and Granule Company in 1886. He decided that so important a medical discovery deserved a trademark, and he proceeded to design one. It looked like this (that's Dr. W. E. P.'s thumb crushing the pill):

Pill-pressing soon became the major activity of the doctor brothers Upjohn. They added color to their pills, a high polish and, of course, a sugar coating. Along with this injection of pharmaceutical elegance, they paid attention to their trademark, occasionally changing it and refining it—but not too severely.

By 1913, Upjohn was busily providing the nation's druggists with fluid extracts, tinctures, elixirs, ointments, syrups and "Phenolax," claimed to be the first candy-type laxative. The time had come to reappraise the slogan boasting that Upjohn's pills could be "reduced to powder under the thumb." A compromise was adopted: the thumb illustration stayed, but the slogan was changed to identify the company as "the originators of friable pills."

Dr. W. E. Upjohn's thumb on the pill remained the brand identificaton until 1945 when the more severe and professional trademark was adopted. Shortly thereafter the company ran its final batch of friable pills, and then abandoned the line for good.

And thus passed a trademark unique in the annals of American industry. Upjohn's original trademark was probably the only one in history that proudly displayed the business as being under the owner's thumb.

## WEBSTER COLOPHON

The name Webster long ago entered the public domain, which means anybody can (and does) use it for dictionaries of all sizes, prices and quality. But there is only one true lineal descendant of the original that can honestly claim a heritage directly rooted in Noah Webster's historic and most extensive unabridged dictionary. This is the dictionary identified by the trademark "A Merriam-Webster" and the trademark symbol (or colophon) shown above.

George and Charles Merriam, two brothers from Springfield, Massachusetts, were responsible for the Merriam end of the hyphenated name. They bought the rights to the dictionary when Noah died in 1843. Four years later, with the help of Noah's son William and son-in-law Chauncey A. Goodrich, they published their first unabridged Merriam-Webster.

Initial appearance of the trademark-colophon was on the monumental *Webster's International Dictionary*, published in 1890. The wreath was of laurel leaves, ancient Greek symbol for crowning achievement; Noah's initials were inscribed in the center as an intertwined N and W.

In time the monogram and wreath were placed inside a larger circle, which also includes *Webster's Seventh New Collegiate Dictionary* or some similar descriptive title.

There is a small footnote to this history: Noah Webster also authored another enormously successful best seller, *The Blue-Backed Speller*. Before its popularity finally waned, over 10,000,000 copies had been sold. But by the early 1900's its fame was fading and it was soon forgotten. Today when somebody says, "Well, according to Webster's . . .," you automatically think dictionary, not spelling book.

## WESTINGHOUSE

What do you see when you look at this trademark? Merely the twenty-third letter of the alphabet? Or a symbol that suggests "a molecular structure, wires and plugs, a wiring diagram, tubes and light bulbs"?

The latter description is by the eminent graphic designer Paul Rand. He created the trademark for Westinghouse. In so doing, he had very specific symbolism in mind to convey the image of this electronic giant. He aimed to make Westinghouse's trademark identify both its owner and the nature of the business as well.

The trademark is far simpler than the five variations that preceded it. The first appeared in the early part of the century; it was a circle enclosing the legend, "The name Westinghouse is a guarantee." Around the black rim was inscribed "Westinghouse Electric."

Within a decade it changed to a plain W in the center, with the words "Westinghouse Electric" in an oblong box under the W—apparently to prevent the W from being read as an upside-down M.

By 1940 "Westinghouse" again appeared on the rim of the circle, and the oblong under the W assumed its present underscore form. In 1953 the "Westinghouse" was dropped, and in 1960—just in time for the company's sponsorship of the political convention telecasts—the present design was adopted. It is usually printed in white against a blue-violet background, which the company calls "Westinghouse blue."

Today the trademark is used in the many countries and territories where the company's representatives are found. In its smallest version—six-thousandths of an inch in diameter and visible only under a 20-power microscope—it appears on the company's molecular electronic devices, probably the world's tiniest trademark. Seventy thousand times larger is the "Circle W" on the front of the Westinghouse transformer plant in Munice, Indiana. This version is as high as a three-story house.

## WHITE OWL CIGARS

How does a cigar get named for an owl—particularly a white owl? Simple: Let a live white owl fly in the window of the man looking for a cigar brand and the deed will be done.

That is what happened in 1867 when a cigar maker named Storm (of Straiton & Storm) was mulling over the problem of a name for his newest creation. As he brooded, a white owl swooped into the bedroom of his Long Island home, solving the dilemma of what to name the new cigar. He called the new line the Owl brand, and in no time at all Owl was a national favorite.

A few years later Straiton & Storm was absorbed by the emerging giant of the cigar business, General Cigar Company. General Cigar liked the name Owl so well that in 1917 it adapted it for its new line of "Invincibles." Only this time the full name was used: White Owl.

Sales of White Owl cigars soon left the old Owl brand way behind—so far behind that plain Owl was dropped and White Owl ruled the roost.

The White Owl label and cigar bands provide a capsule economic history of America. In 1930 the printed price was 7 cents, three for 20 cents. A year later the Depression knocked the label price down to 6 cents, then to a nickel in 1933. That year the owl shared his labels with the blue eagle of NRA (National Recovery Administration) and the Chicago World's Fair.

In 1946, post-war prosperity and inflation set in; the label was redone with a two-for-15-cents imprint. Inflation struck hard in 1957, and White Owl became a 10-cent cigar. And in 1963, the line expanded to include four cigars that sold for two for a quarter and one that sold for three for 32 cents.

Through it all the bird has perched proudly on band and box.

## WHITE ROCK'S PSYCHE

Her measurements are 35-25-35. She's named for a Greek beauty who had the good fortune to be mistaken for Aphrodite, the goddess of love and beauty. And she's been kneeling on that rock for nigh on to 77 years.

The girl is White Rock's Psyche. She had her genesis in a rather Rabelasian piece of art displayed at the 1893 World's Columbian Exposition in Chicago (her measurements then were 37-27-38). The artist, Paul Thumann, called it "Psyche at Nature's Mirror."

His inspiration was the legend of the beautiful maid who fell in love with Eros, the Greek version of Cupid. Following a series of earthly and heavenly mis- adventures, Psyche finally won the approval of Venus, mother of Eros, and achieved immortality through the special dispensation of Zeus. Her butterfly wings are intended to convey this state of immortality.

The transition to a sensational trademark resulted from a visit to the fair by the owners of the young White Rock Mineral Springs Company, whose business was the sale and bottling of a mineral water flowing in Waukesha, Wisconsin. They were on the lookout for a trademark that symbolized purity and quality. Psyche filled the bill very well.

She has enjoyed a zestful, eye-filling life ever since. She has been the subject of cartoon art (Wife, finding Psyche helping husband mix drinks in kitchen, says, "What are you two up to?"). On occasion, she has left the rock entirely or been about to leave—such as the time an ad for White Rock Vodka Mix showed her poised to plunge. In a burst of delayed modesty, the company's 1960 version made Psyche appear somewhat more demure.

A few years back the company ran a contest for the best three-word slogan to go along with Psyche. The winner was "Ah, so pure!" Among the rejects were "My knees hurt" and "You're staring, Melvin."

## WHITMAN'S MESSENGER

Look at any collection of famous samplers and you're likely to see animals, utensils, seashells, birdhouses, flowers, tombstones, coats of arms, windmills, Biblical quotations, and maybe the man in the moon—but nary a picture of a box of candy. Nevertheless, a box of candy—Whitman's Sampler with its Messenger Boy— has helped keep the memory of samplers alive.

Whitman's had been in business 70 years before it hit on the sampler device to promote its chocolates. The year was 1912. A special box consisting of a "personalized selection" of chocolates was planned. The question was, How to bring it to public attention?

The company president had long admired a family sampler heirloom. He commissioned a piece of needlework with authentic sampler motifs to be used as the design for the package. The resulting design is still seen today in drugstores, candy shops, department stores, etc., all over the land.

The Messenger Boy came along three years later, when it was registered as a companion trademark to the sampler design. He appears on just about every piece of stationery and advertising matter used by the company; Whitman salesmen use business cards cut in the shape of the Messenger Boy.

The company is not without gratitude to the girls and women of olden days who inspired its sampler package. As a testimonial to them, it maintains on permanent display a collection of about 600 samplers "of exceptionally delicate workmanship and unusual pictorial interest" produced between 1790 and 1840, the golden age of samplery.

## WOOLMARK

In 1964 the swirling figure of the "Woolmark" was unknown. Today it's recognized all over the world. Thousands of manufacturers use it to promote the sale of clothing, blankets, carpets and other wool products.

Behind this unusual success story is one of the most inspired trademark promotional campaigns ever devised. The problem was simple enough: Early in the 1960's the world's wool growers faced up to the brutal reality that synthetic fibers were becoming a very serious threat. Wool consumption was dropping. Millions of consumers (mainly younger ones) were becoming indifferent to wool's traditional image as a top-quality product.

The International Wool Secretariat, headquartered in London, represents the great wool-growing industries of Australia, New Zealand and South Africa. To IWS went the job of refurbishing wool's image.

It launched a global design competition for a symbol that would do for wool what the sterling mark has done for silver—something that would be recognized everywhere as a sign of quality for wool products conforming to the association's standards. It would have to be universal, its use not inhibited by language or national barriers.

The judges' choice was a design by Italian artist Francesco Saroglia. Saroglia's swirl conveyed "constant movement symbolizing both the timelessness of wool and its modernity in the space age."

Nearly 10,000 companies are licensed to use the Woolmark, and they put it on 120,000,000 labels a year. Surveys testify to the campaign's success—in some countries eight out of ten shoppers know what the symbol means. That's not bad for a trademark that's a mere seven years old.

## MR. ZIP

The origins of Mr. Zip go back a dozen years or so when Chase Manhattan Bank of New York was running a lighthearted campaign to promote its bank-by-mail service. Cunningham & Walsh was the ad agency involved. The art director, Howard Wilcox, headed the design group that laid out the ads. One of its efforts was a poster with a couplet reading "In rain or hail/ Bank by mail." The poster needed an illustration, and Wilcox—whose father was a retired postmaster—created a figure he describes as done in a "naive, childlike style," depicting a postman delivering a letter.

The drawing was used a couple of times, then filed away. About five years later the Post Office Department queried the American Telephone and Telegraph Company for ideas on how to get fast public acceptance of its new postal zone system. One of AT&T's ad agencies was Cunningham & Walsh, and there someone remembered Wilcox's sprightly sketch of a postman on the move. AT&T acquired it and presented it to the Post Office Department.

The whimsical figure was a natural. Post Office artists retained the face but sharpened up the limbs and torso

191

and added a mailbag. Says Wilcox: "They gave it the cartoon treatment."

At first the figure was called "Mr. P.O. Zone." But the name was soon changed to "Mr. ZIP." (ZIP stands for Zone Improvement Program.)

Most trademarks or symbols need many years to win much recognition. But not Mr. ZIP. Within four or five years the Post Office found 80% of the public knew what he stood for. It's the kind of instant recognition that puts Mr. ZIP right up there with Smokey the Bear.